THE RISE OF PROTESTANT MONASTICISM

THE RISE OF PROTESTANT MONASTICISM

by

François Biot, O.P.

translated by

W. J. Kerrigan

HELICON

BALTIMORE · DUBLIN

1963

Helicon Press, Inc.
1120 N. Calvert Street
Baltimore, Maryland, 21202

Helicon Limited
53 Capel Street
Dublin 1, Ireland

Library of Congress Catalog Card Number 63-1940

Nihil Obstat: CARROLL E. SATTERFIELD
Censor Librorum

Imprimatur: ✠LAWRENCE J. SHEHAN, D.D.
Archbishop of Baltimore
August 14, 1963

The *Nihil Obstat* and *Imprimatur* are official declarations that a book or pamphlet is free of doctrinal or moral error. No implication is contained therein that those who have granted the *Nihil Obstat* and *Imprimatur* agree with the opinions expressed.

First Edition

PRINTED IN THE REPUBLIC OF IRELAND BY
HELY THOM LIMITED, DUBLIN

To

Father Paul Couturier

in memoriam

Contents

THE RISE OF PROTESTANT MONASTICISM

INTRODUCTION

THE movement towards Christian unity will one day prove to have been a keynote in the spiritual development of the twentieth century. This ecumenical movement arose some fifty years ago out of the peculiar requirements of missionary work. At first limited to a few specialists, it has spread in widening circles among Protestant and certain Eastern Churches. And it is now over ten years since the founding of the World Council of Churches made the importance of this movement clear.

Catholics as well, even if sometimes hesitantly, have begun to take part in it. By his outspoken anxiety for Christian unity and by his convocation of the general council, Pope John XXIII has awakened all the faithful of the Church of Rome to the tragedy of disunion and to the need for unity. And these faithful are viewing their separated brethren, Protestants in especial, with quickened interest.

This interest, it must be recognized however, is liable to run to either of equally destructive extremes. On the one hand, because of scrupulous and unimaginative fidelity to the teachings of the Church, some of the faithful may misunderstand and hence undervalue what is worthwhile in the separated Churches, Protestant in especial. Or on the other hand, eager to find common boundaries for purposes of communication, others are tempted to minimize the real distances which separate them from other Christian creeds—again, Protestant-ism in especial. Principally, they may tend to exaggerate the importance of certain items (like possession of a liturgy, sacraments, and religious communities) which make some Protestant Churches today resemble the Catholic Church.

1

Recognizing the danger of those extremes, we should like in this brief study of Protestant religious communities to facilitate Protestant–Catholic communication at one particular and quite significant point. That is, we wish to show how Protestantism today has in some instances concretely accepted the principle of religious community life, and to give recognition to the value—spiritual and Christian—of the communities that have resulted from this acceptance. Yet at the same time we intend to indicate exactly how far this rediscovery of common religious life has proceeded.

Since it is a rediscovery, our first task will be to show how monastic and religious communities disappeared in Protestant life as a result of sixteenth-century Reformation attitudes towards them. Of course, in doing this we cannot undertake to present here all that the Reformers said and wrote on the subject, nor even to outline the position of each and every sixteenth-century Protestant author. But we believe that the resultant selection that is forced upon us will sufficiently demonstrate the Reformation's rejection of monasticism —a rejection that became concrete when with few exceptions, the Churches born of the Reform undertook to suppress monasteries and convents.

After this treatment of the attitude of the Reformers, we shall describe some Protestant religious communities existing in France, in French-speaking countries, and in Germany today. The reader will perhaps be surprised that some descriptions are prefaced by historical accounts: of a convent or monastery falling within the ambit of the Reformation in the sixteenth century and continuing its existence under a "Protestant" rule for some decades, or of a Pietist experiment later, or of the foundation of Deaconesses in the nineteenth century. Yet such accounts are useful for presenting in perspective the renewal of religious community life in the present day.

Nor should the reader be surprised that we have chosen to treat only a few, well-established contemporary communities. For our purposes we need not list all of them, much less all of the experiments in community living which Protestantism furnishes today. It will suffice to present several examples and to describe these in such detail that Protestant resumption of religious community life can be shown in full color.

More than one reader will be surprised, of course, at our leaving completely aside the Anglican communities, for they are comparatively numerous, and some of them have been well tried by the test of time. But the reason for our leaving them aside is simple: we feel that Anglicanism is an original Christian faith which it would be quite wrong to classify as Protestant. If the Church of England comprises numerous Protestant elements, and if certain periods of its history are marked by the preponderance of such elements, still it comprises numerous and important Catholic elements as well, kept since the sixteenth century, whose influence has constantly expanded in the whole of the Anglican Communion since the Oxford Movement. To classify Anglicanism under the head of Protestantism is thus an error and an injustice.[1]

In a final section we shall try to show the fundamental reasons for the existence of Protestant religious communities. Here the reader will have to keep in mind that there is no official Protestant doctrine on the religious life. Among these communities themselves there is no unanimity in the reasons they give to justify their existence. Certain elements of a consensus, however, do exist in nearly every case, even if they are not always quite explicit; and these elements we shall undertake to reveal.

Various publications of the communities themselves have been of great help to us in this undertaking, especially the publications of some of the Brothers of Taizé. Of course, neither on these nor on other matters does there exist, in a community like Taizé, any common theological teaching, for the brothers who are theologians are not charged with exercising a doctrinal authority over the community. But it does seem to us that these brothers have succeeded in putting into words objectives shared by their confreres. On these grounds we have felt justified in utilizing their formulations.

The reader will notice that these theologically formulated justifications are of later birth than the concrete communities they seek to explain. In fact, quite often the founders and first members of the Protestant communities of today did not know beforehand all that religious community life had in store for them nor, to tell the truth, all that it would reveal to them. These justifications then, these express reasons and motives, often have their basis in practical

---

1 Anglican communities form the subject of quite numerous existing works. To cite but one of the most important in the present connection: Peter F. Anson, *The Call of the Cloister*, S.P.C.K., London, 1956.

experience. This is of an importance that we hope the reader will not overlook.

Finally, we have limited the scope of this book to a simple reporting of the facts. Our objective is to make known to Catholic people the importance and the value of the Protestant religious-community movement. It is outside our scope here to form in any way the judgment of Catholics on religious and monastic life, or on Protestantism. Accordingly, in regard both to the facts of Protestant community life and to the theological or other justifications given for that life, we have abstained from giving any judgment, any appraisal, or in fact any Catholic point of view. Often, indeed, not to have so abstained would have involved long explanations of a sort out of place here. Readers, then, must bear in mind this abstention which we have imposed upon ourself, in the first part of the book especially.

In the same way, as regards the Reformers' negative attitude towards monastic life and their sometimes quite violent criticism of it, we have not marshaled the whole battery of replies available on the Catholic side, though we have indicated the fundamental grounds for them. To the Reformers' rejection of monastic life, current Protestant adoption of that life furnishes a concrete reply, and theological justification of it a doctrinal one. Here we shall simply essay to present both current practice and current theory as objectively as possible.

In the present-day quest for unity—in the world's progress towards the realization of the promise implicit in Christ's prayer—Protestant religious communities will have, we believe, an important role to fill. The principal aim of this present volume is to describe that role and at the same time to point out one feasible direction for the ecumenical movement, namely, the rediscovery of important elements in the life of the Church through meditation and through grave consideration of the New Testament and its requirements. May the Catholic reader find in the concrete testimony furnished by his separated brothers in these religious communities an invitation and an example; for he, too, is called upon to work for Christian unity, and he needs in this work the encouraging example of these brothers' ecumenical fervor.

Since our purpose is to show in the current Protestant religious revival a new element that breaks with at least one Protestant attitude or tradition, our first task will consist in making clear what we mean by the Protestantism to which this element is something new. In our use of the term, Protestantism is a form of Western Christianity distinct from Roman Catholicism on the one hand and from Anglicanism on the other, as well as from the much more recent sectary movements. It was born in the sixteenth century of the dogmatic and practical positions adopted by a certain number of major "prophets," the Reformers. It is, then, these men's opinion of monasticism and of the religious life in general that we must first determine. For the phenomenon of monasticism and of life under religious rule had too great importance in the Church of the sixteenth century for either party to avoid expressing, under the stress of various circumstances, their thought on the subject. It is certain, as well, that monasticism and conventualism are too closely bound up with Christian life for a "reform" of the latter not to have immediate and explicit consequences for the former.

The Reformers' criticisms of monastic life were extremely severe, as the reader will see clearly in the pages that follow. But their criticisms comprised elements of various kinds, and profoundly just religious perceptions were joined to controversy careless of objectivity. In the interests of honest reporting we have sought here neither to sweeten nor to dilute the documents which the pioneers of the Reformation have left us. We have even followed the plan of presenting the various arguments advanced in those texts without the intrusion of viewpoints with which Catholic theological teaching could confront those arguments. (It has in fact not neglected to confront them ever since the sixteenth century by means of the writings of theologians, some of whom have been very able.)

The reader, therefore, must keep in mind that the arguments brought into play by the Reformers, however violent these arguments and however closely connected with a just assessment of the facts, have not gone without an answer. But he also must not forget all the shortcomings and all the abuses which had crept into religious life and which no one could seriously think of defending against the attacks, in this case justified, of the Reformers.

Part One

THE POSITION OF THE REFORMERS ON

RELIGIOUS AND MONASTIC LIFE

Chapter I

LUTHER'S POSITION

THE Reformation began, as everyone knows, October 31, 1517. That is when Martin Luther, a young professor at the University of Wittenberg, fastened his ninety-five theses on the value of indulgences to the door of All Saints' church in Wittenberg. The date is a symbolic one. In posting his theses, the young doctor of divinity had doubtless no other intention than to provoke a theological discussion on the subject of indulgences—but no discussion followed. What did follow had quite a different bearing on the history of the Church!

Now this young doctor Martin Luther[1] was a monk of the order of the Hermits of Saint Augustine. This order, whose beginnings are supposed to go back to Saint Augustine himself, was one which had been unified by a decision of the Holy See. On April 9, 1256, Pope Alexander IV had regrouped the different bodies of hermits claiming Saint Augustine as their founder into four provinces, under the authority of a single prior general. Later, at the end of the sixteenth century, the Hermits of Saint Augustine seem to have been quite flourishing, with about two thousand convents. Doubtless, the decadence of the time must have affected the Hermits of Saint Augustine as it did the greater part of orders of monks properly speaking, or of mendicants. However that may be, the convent which Martin Luther entered on July 17, 1505, at Erfurt, formed a part of the "observance." The religious life led there was a serious one, even austere. The convent was poor, the members often suffering, it seems, from cold and from hunger.

---

1 For the history of Luther, his monastic years in especial, one may consult Professor J. Lortz's work, *Die Reformation in Deutschland*, I, 147–192.

7

Why had Martin Luther, as a young student at the university, decided to enter religion? His decision, we know, was an abrupt one. His own account of the matter later would ascribe it to a vow to become a monk which he made when frightened during a storm by a bolt of lightning striking quite close to him. Though it seems that this explanation is to be taken with some reservation, there can be no doubt that Luther entered the convent with good and worthy motives. His time as a postulant and his year as a novice must have been spent responsibly in a religious house where, such was the severity of the daily rule of life, no one could become fully fledged without well-tested fitness for membership. It is unthinkable, of course, that his stay as a postulant and as a novice was a forced one; and it was of his own free will that, in 1506, he made his perpetual vows. A year later, he was ordained a priest. Such was the confidence of his religious superiors in his sincerity that he was then enrolled as a theology student destined for professorship.

It is extremely difficult to gain any exact knowledge of the quality of Friar Martin's religious life during the years 1505–1517. The historical value of his own frequent allusions to the period—notably in his *Table Talk*—is thoroughly relative, for not only was Luther reviewing those years under the influence of an intervening profound religious experience and development, but also his hatred for everything "Popish" offers little guarantee of objectivity.

What does seem certain at least is that the convent at Erfurt must have insisted on penitential exercises: fasting (a hundred sixty days out of the year, without meat or milk products); scourging one's self; going without much sleep. That insistence, however, cannot have obscured Luther's essential understanding of such practices—if not when he first took the habit at least when he made perpetual vows. Mortification was practiced to free men to undergo the action of God: "May he accomplish in you what he has begun in you" was the prior's welcome on the day of Luther's entrance to the convent.

For another thing, in the life of the convent at Erfurt the reading of the Scriptures played a large part. To each religious was assigned his personal copy of the Bible, and we know that Luther read and reread his during his years as a religious.

Such advice as Luther received from his novice master, from his spiritual director, and from Staupitz[2] emphasized surrender of self to Jesus Christ, rather than any kind of religious activism. To this particular young monk who yearned to appease the religious anguish caused by his conception of the exactions and the sovereign power of God, his spiritual fathers spoke not so much of penance, of mortification, and of praying as of abandoning himself to the redemptive graces purchased for him by Christ. But there is no doubt that Friar Martin was simply so much absorbed in his particular personal problem that he was hardly able to attend to the counsel and advice of others. He was going to have to come to a personal conviction of salvation in order to find, as he put it, peace.

What the stages were in the development of his attitude towards religious life after he did reach that conviction it is difficult to discern clearly. In his *Commentary on the Epistle to the Romans* (1515–1516) Luther seems already to have advanced theories hardly conformable to traditional doctrine. But it does not seem that at this period he had yet given up religious life. (As a matter of fact Luther had in effect left the Church before he severed relations with his religious order.) It is true that in February, 1518, the new superior general of the Augustinians was requested by Pope Leo X to try to calm down this young Augustinian, Martin Luther. And yet, on the other hand, in the following May of the same year, Luther was still highly enough esteemed in his own order to be accepted as a participant in the theological panel for the general chapter.

It is certain that even at the time of the Leipzig dispute (1519) Luther's attitude on religious life was still quite affirmative, as a sermon of his on baptism[3] in the autumn of 1519 bears witness. In it Luther expressed his convictions about the value of religious vows and their connection with baptism. To implement, he said, the operation of baptism, which is our liberation from sin, God instituted several means, such as life as a marriage partner, life as a religious, and life as a parish priest. He was convinced, of course, that baptismal vows surpass in importance and in value those whereby one be-

---

2 Staupitz from 1503 to 1520 was vicar general of the Augustinian order in Germany. He was therefore the young Friar Martin's superior; and it was Staupitz who entrusted Luther with a chair at the University of Wittenberg.

3 Cf. *Quatemember, Evangelische Jahresbriefe*, IV (1956–1957), pp. 226–228.

comes a religious. But baptismal vows do not leave religious vows without any value; nor do they mean that becoming a religious is not a legitimate choice. In fact, he goes on to say, as a means for implementing the operation of baptism, religious life in itself is better than marriage: it is a way at once straighter, shorter, and requiring one to follow more closely in the footsteps of Christ. In itself, life in an order is a better way of promoting the effects of baptism than any other. Thus, while criticizing vigorously the religious orders existing in his day, Luther gave recognition in this sermon on baptism to the legitimate function of religious life in the road to salvation. Community life established by vows had, then, a perfect right to exist within the organism of the Church, and could not be considered at odds with the ordinances of the Scriptures.

Some months later, in June, 1520, the bull *Exsurge Domine* excommunicated Luther. At once he wrote in short order three papers which compose as it were the manifesto of the Reformation: *To the Christian Nobility of the German Nation on the Betterment of the Christian Condition; On the Babylonian Captivity of the Church* (in Latin); and *On the Liberty of a Christian Man.* It is in the first of these papers that we find interesting news on the vows.

This paper, as we know, clearly proclaims the universal priesthood of all Christians, there being no priestly state distinct from the lay state. Different vocations exist, however, which set up within the Church a special division. As it turns out, with their special calling clerics have to live a special kind of life willed by God himself, and this involves their being unmarried. Now this celibacy is purely of human institution. Furthermore, it is not even (properly speaking) the object of a vow, but is implicitly understood when one receives the order of subdiaconate. This celibacy, Luther therefore argues, is not binding; and clerics who have been living with mistresses ought plainly and simply to get married, in spite of laws from Rome.

In contrast, so far as the religious life (which is quite another calling) went, Luther's attitudes at that moment were still definitely the classic ones: a man obviously must keep his promises and his bargains. And Luther began now to envisage a reformation of religious life which would retain the value of a perpetual commitment.

But it must be recognized that to call into question the commitment to celibacy implied in the subdiaconate meant to call into account

before long the worth of the vows as well. Beginning with this year
1520, then, a certain number of events led Luther to take up this
problem again, and to bring his broad reformative intuitions to bear
on the question of these monastic vows and on the life of religion.

Early in 1521 the case of a cleric who had taken a wife came up
before the jurists of the University of Wittenberg. Philipp Melanchthon seized the opportunity to take up the defense of the accused,
his brief being immediately published in Latin and in German. In it
Melanchthon demonstrated that by divine law the marriage of clerics
is permissible. He argued that the history of the Church shows what
resistance was met by the introduction of ecclesiastical celibacy. As a
purely human institution, this ought to bind only in the measure that
it is possible—and a fortiori because it is not the object of a vow
properly speaking.

Two similar businesses fell out about the same time involving the
question of ecclesiastical celibacy. Very quickly the worth of the vows
as well was questioned, and the fat was in the fire.

In June of 1521 Andreas von Bodenstein of Karlstadt entered into
the discussion. On June 29 he published seven propositions, in which
he treated together the question of the celibacy of clerics and the
question of monastic vows. According to Bodenstein, in compliance
with 1 Tim 5:9 ("If a woman is to be put on the list of widows, she
must have reached, at least, the age of sixty, and have been faithful
to one husband") one ought to refuse to ordain to the priesthood all
who are not married! As for monks, he was of the opinion that they,
too, ought to get married if they found themselves assailed by too
many problems in remaining chaste: their marriage would be a sin,
of course, but less a sin than that of weltering in obscene lust.

Through the agency of Melanchthon, these Karlstadt propositions
came to the attention of Luther at the end of July. He declared himself in basic agreement with them. But in the correspondence which
followed between Melanchthon and Luther, we find Luther looking
for better scriptural supports than 1 Tim 5:9, which he felt was far
from satisfactory. On the celibacy of clerics, it seemed to him that
1 Tim 4:3 was excellent: in that passage St. Paul criticizes those who
forbid marriage. But on the question of monastic vows Luther had
found nothing yet which appeared to him really decisive.

A disputation was held at the end of July in Wittenberg on the subject of monastic life. During this time Melanchthon prepared the initial instalment of his *Loci Theologici*, in which he takes up among other things the question of monastic vows.

Melanchthon saw no recommendation of the vows in the Scriptures. Indeed, the vows virtually create a state of spiritual slavery irreconcilable with the evangelical liberty of the true Christian. Human weakness, for its part, seems less than an invitation to be making vows. Besides, why make special vows of poverty, obedience, and chastity? Every Christian is bound to possess nothing for his own sake but to place everything, through charity, at the disposition of others; every Christian must live freely according to his state of life and his calling; and finally, every Christian in his personal situation must be pure and chaste. True enough, Christ himself had given his recommendation to the single life, but he had done so to only a very small number.

In the *Loci* Melanchthon did not treat of the bond created by a vow. But in a letter to Luther he declared that a person is no longer bound by his vows from the moment that he finds it impossible to keep them. This point was received by Luther with some hesitancy. Would not this principle be applicable also to the Ten Commandments, which would not oblige then in case of impossibility? And what of marriage? Its indissolubility would then be conditioned by the possibility of living within its bonds.

Thus several days after, on September 9, Luther was sufficiently re-engaged with the problem to produce titles for a series of theses that were published during the days that followed: these are the *Themata de votis*. On October 8 they were dispatched to Wittenberg, where the effect they produced was sensational. Bugenhaven, they say, cried out, "This business has the powder in it to blow up the country, such as no doctrine before these theses has ever had." Addressed to "the bishops and deacons of the Church of Wittenberg," they elicited the enthusiasm of some, the strong disapproval of others.

From this moment on, work after work was to come from the pen of Luther on the subject of religious life and the vows. November 21, 1521, he finished his treatise *De votis monasticis Martini Lutherii judicium*, to be published in the latter weeks of February, 1522. April 10, 1523, Luther resumed this subject in his letter to L. Koppe, "Why may religious leave the convent?" March 2, 1523, he sent to

Count Mansfeld his *History of a Cloistered Religious Nobleman;*
May 18, 1526, he communicated to Prince John Frederick of Saxony
answers on a certain number of scriptural texts which had been submitted to him concerning the vows. During October and November
of 1528 he wrote a commentary on a piece composed by an ex-nun
on her reasons for leaving the convent. Finally, June 13, 1530, he
sent an answer to a person of high rank, on the question of monastic
vows.

But his work of unrivaled importance is his *De votis monasticis
judicium.* Luther himself in fact, was to retain a particular esteem for
it, and later he would refer to it anyone who asked him his opinion
on the vows. Yet this work was an improvisation: after the publication of the theses, which produced so lively an impression in university circles at Wittenberg, Luther retired to Wartburg, where, amid
all sorts of other labors, he very rapidly penned this treatise. While
on November 1 he wrote of his projects to one of his friends at
Strassburg with no mention of this text, yet no later than November
21 he was winding it up with the dedication to his father. He sent
the manuscript to Spalatin,[4] who kept it hidden, and it was only
upon renewed insistence from Luther that Spalatin surrendered it
for printing.

The treatise then spread very rapidly. In March of 1522 it was
printed at Basle; in June, a first translation appeared in German, by
Leo Juds. Sometime after June 13 a new edition was produced at
Wittenberg, with some modifications and additions by the author;
before the end of 1522 Justin Jodas had published his German
version.

The success of the work is further illustrated by the number of
publications which appeared in response to Luther's criticism. In
1522 and during the years following, a whole series of works attacked
Luther's attitudes on the religious life and attempted with varying
degrees of success to refute them. Despite these attacks, it does seem
—quite apart from legendary exaggerations—that many monks, and
nuns, and religious of all descriptions, were "freed" by the word of
Luther. They believed themselves authorized, nay even bound in

---

4 Spalatin's real name was George Burkhardt. He had been born in Spalt, near
Nuremburg. He was chaplain and secretary to Luther's protector, Prince-
Elector Frederick the Wise.

conscience, to leave their convents and often to contract marriage. In the personal case of Luther, however, we know that matters did not take so brisk a turn, for upon presenting his treatise to the vicar of the Augustinians, W. Link, and indicating to the vicar that his position on the religious life was to be found therein, he took the trouble to add: "As for me, I shall remain in this habit and in this way of life."

Despite its first success it must be said that the *De votis* has not maintained a place among the works of Luther habitually cited today. It is relatively little and imperfectly known. In France it is practically ignored: there has not been a French translation of it since those which go back to the time of its first appearance. And yet, on the authority of a man like Otto Scheel, one of the most celebrated "Lutherologians," who has himself written a commentary on the *De votis,*

> it is to be numbered among the most powerful and most gripping that the pen of Luther produced. It leaves upon an attentive reader a lasting impression of dialectical power, of complete frankness, of high serious-ness, of responsibility, and of strong piety.[5]

The *De votis*[6] seems to be a thoroughly systematic treatise. In fact Luther must have taken considerable pains over a well-thought-out plan for it:

1. The vows are contrary to the word of God; they have no scriptural support in their favor.

2. The vows are contrary to faith, since they are held by the monks to be sources of sanctification.

3. The vows are contrary to evangelical liberty—liberty of con-science—which should be bound by no obligation.

4. The vows are contrary to the commandments of God, for they suppose the existence of "counsels," which in Luther's eyes were

---

5 Cited by H. Esnault, in *Etudes théologiques et religieuses,* No. 1, p. 23. This number as well as No. 3 of the same year printed the beginning of a study by Esnault: "Le *De votis monasticis* de Martin Luther"; unfortunately the continua-tion of this study has not yet appeared.

6 The *De votis monasticis* is to be found in Volume VIII of the critical edition of the complete works of Luther, called the *Weimar* (*WA*), pp. 573–669. Our effort here is to present Luther's thought as it is found in his treatise, without refuting it; this does not mean that we accept responsibility for the German Reformer's allegations.

additions to the commandments. Especially are they contrary to charity, in creating within the Church a state wherein the aim is to be served rather than to serve.

5. The vows are contrary to reason, because of their irrevocability.

A final chapter re-examines the three vows—poverty, obedience, and chastity—contrasting them with the real virtues designated by those names. The vows, instead of promoting these, are detrimental to them.

A few notes on St. Paul's treatment of the subject of widows close this last chapter.

1. The vows are contrary to the word of God.

Beyond any doubt, the perilousness of a monastic vow is bespoken by the fact that it can claim for itself in the Scriptures neither authority nor example. Both in the New Testament and in the primitive Church we find utterly no knowledge of the practice of making any vow whatsoever, but in fact a disapproval of a perpetual vow—rare and quasi-miraculous in any case—of chastity. Vows on system are a purely human and a pernicious invention.

Such was Luther's first categorical assertion.

The reasoning behind it is no less clearly set forth: According to the New Testament, Christ is the one and only way to salvation. Everything apart from Jesus Christ, everything to the right or to the left of this living Way, is to be rejected.

Now it was precisely the vows that pretended to add something to the Gospel and to Christ. Religious orders, with their rules, were proposing themselves as ways to salvation—in fact as better routes than the ordinary way. True enough, monastic life did look for justification to the distinction between the "commandments" and the "counsels." For ordinary Christians, it was sufficient to follow the commandments; for monks, it was necessary to follow the "evangelical counsels" as well, and to these they bound themselves by vow, thinking this way better and surer than the "ordinary" way. In other words, not all of the Gospel is for all; in part it contains directions, in part simply advice.

But Luther wanted none of this distinction, which did not seem to him at all attested by the New Testament. In reality, what was found in the Bible, and was called "counsel" by monks and their defenders, was purely and simply precept. And even if one were to agree with the monks' hypothesis of the existence of evangelical counsels, one would see that for the monks themselves these counsels became precepts. To cling still to the idea of the existence of "counsels" would be to find one's self opposed to what one believed came from Christ himself.

This was true particularly of the vow of chastity or of virginity. If a gratuitous single state was counseled by the New Testament—and this within the limits emphasized by Luther—the same was not true of a vow of celibacy, which turned a freely chosen counsel into a precept and thus presumed to go beyond the requirements of the Gospel. So it was with obedience: the New Testament required Christians to submit to one another. Here there was no question of any submission vowed to a single personage—and vowed moreover in matters expressly specified according to the rule of a religious community.

Thus, then, to review briefly this last point: the vows were contrary to the word of God, because they established a *particular* and *superior* way, one different from the Gospel way, which is to say different, finally, from the way of the one and only Mediator.

2. The vows are contrary to faith.

As everyone knows, Luther's great positive assertion, the one that seemed to him himself to be his essential rediscovery, was "justification by faith alone." All the deeds, however difficult or even heroic they might be, that man could perform before justification were utterly incapable of "justifying" him, sinner that he was and remained.

The same was true even of works which man might perform after his "justification" but without faith, that is, the works whereby he might think to present himself as "just" in the sight of God. Even in this case man would have to be said to be spurning the one true source of justification—faith.

Now precisely this kind of works, at least with the exception of the case of a "miraculous" protection, were constituted by the vows. That was the point that Luther was here proposing, in noting among others the following:

a) By the vows, monks "abolished" the grace of baptism. In fact, they thought of making their profession (i.e., taking the vows that signify formal acceptance of life in a religious order) as a second baptism. Luther here alluded to a theory which thought of religious profession as an act of perfect love that restored the state of innocence conferred by baptism, and thus to that extent was like another baptism. But taken absolutely, as Luther seemed to take it here, the theory quite overlooked the unique properties of baptism as the sacrament of "justification."

b) When monks took vows, they did so because they thought to make themselves thereby pleasing to God; that is, they wished thus to become good and just and to appear so in the eyes of God. They maintained that to this sanctity their poverty, chastity, and obedience were not only sure ways, but even better ways than the ones pursued by the rank and file of the faithful.

c) As if this were not enough, through these vows they thought to become, themselves, a source of sanctification for others. In seeking to aid others by their works and by their merits, they were considering themselves like Christ. Here Luther had in mind the spiritual bond taken as a basis for third orders, oblateships, and the like: associations of lay people who sought to share in the merits and graces of one or other religious order, to which they attached themselves for the inspiration provided by the spirituality, ascetic methods, and other religious activities of that particular order.

As a consequence, save for miraculous cases—St. Bernard, or even St. Francis—whoever made the religious profession was declaring to God something tantamount to this:

> Behold, O God, I vow to you to be no longer a Christian; I revoke the vow made at my baptism; no longer shall Christ be my support, and no longer shall I live in him. All that is past, outmoded, worthless. Beyond Christ, outside Christ, I make to you a new and better vow: I seek a life in my own works of poverty, chastity, and obedience, and in the works prescribed by this rule. Through these works, in fact, I shall become just, I shall be saved, and I shall make myself profitable to others, for their justice, their salvation.

Luther's verdict here, as we have noted, left room for a miraculous agreement between faith and the vows. At the end of the chapter he stated what a religious profession conformable with faith ought to be:

O God, I vow to you to live in this way, not because I believe it is a way to justice, to salvation, or to forgiveness of sin. . . . That would be an offense to Christ, my Lord, because it would be a denial of his merits. . . . But since I must live on this earth, and since I must not be idle while here, I have chosen this manner of life in order to put my body to use, to render service to my fellow man, and to make God's word my meditation, just as others choose tilling the soil, or some other daily employment.[7]

3. The vows are contrary to evangelical liberty.

At the time when Luther was writing his *De votis monasticis judicium*, he had already published some very important texts on Christian liberty, especially the treatise *Von der Freiheit eines Chris-tenmenschen*, in 1520. In the *De votis*, he reviewed this question of liberty more briefly. For him, to assert the liberty of a Christian man was only a new way of proclaiming that faith is the sole source of justification. In the face of human works—even those commanded by God—Christian conscience was free to the extent that it placed no confidence in them, but only in the works of Christ. A Christian was bound to keep the commandments of God and perform "the works of faith," but this was not out of obligation, nor necessary for salvation (as if salvation were to be found in the performance of human works). They were done in a state of freedom, viewing these works as the simple fruits of faith (since without these one's faith would not be authentic).

In theory, doubtless—Luther began by conceding—the vows could be kept in that way. In the state of spiritual liberty, that is, they could be kept freely and gratuitously, for the utility and advantage of one's fellow men. They could be viewed as Christ's operations in man, gifts ascribable to him, without there being seen in them any "satisfaction" for sin, or any moral or spiritual superiority.

In practice, however, this ideal was attainable only by a miracle, by those who were led interiorly and were safeguarded by the Spirit of Christ. Apart from these miraculous and—the context forces us to understand—almost chimerical conditions, the vows were not kept in a state of religious liberty. For those who made the vows (as for those who defended them theologically) they constituted a kind of

---

7 *WA*, VIII, p. 603, ll. 15–20.

life superior to the ordinary Christian one. But this superiority could not have been based on faith, for by this measure any one way of life was equal to any other. Whatever the degree of heroism they might involve, each of them was just as much incapable as any other of contributing any of the positive elements of justification. The vaunted superiority, then, was based upon works. Consequently, the conscience of a monk who had pronounced these vows was bound to these works and was thus no longer under the rule of liberty.

Besides, the theoretical hypothesis—and, as just shown, this ended by placing the vows and a Christian's liberty in opposition—became patently unacceptable upon analysis: the vows could not be classified as precepts of God. In fact, the obligations born of the vows were purely human in themselves—unlike the precepts with which it had been sought to classify them. The vows transformed into laws, laws purely human, what the Gospel of Christ had left free; they produced occasions of sin exactly where Christ had left Christians at liberty. They were, therefore, a direct offense against the very liberty granted men by Christ.

Finally, the vows were betrayed by their origin to be contrary to spiritual liberty, according to Luther. At the beginning, monasteries had been schools of spiritual education in which disciples lived at liberty in order to learn to live as Christians. Little by little the discipline of the monasteries grew galling to the disciples. To keep them there, this system of pressure had to be contrived: they were made to make promises whereby they obliged themselves in the sight of God to stay in the monastery. Such had been the origin of the vows; clearly it had nothing of the Gospel about it.

Since the vows were opposed to the very liberty which Christ had granted his followers, they had no value for a real Christian. They were null and void, and therefore religious might, in full confidence, leave their way of life, marry, and make money. But Luther felt it necessary to add—recalling doubtless the difficulties he had himself experienced in the face of analogous conclusions when, several years earlier, his friend Melanchthon had presented them to him—that a Christian was not free in marriage in the same fashion that he was free in religious life. The obligation contracted in marriage bound him to another human person, and not directly to God. God had intended that the relationship between justified men and himself should be characterized by liberty, but not that this same liberty should characterize the relationships of these men among one another.

4. The vows are opposed to the commandments of God.

Since the vows were contrary to faith, it was prima facie clear that by this very fact they were in disagreement with the commandments of the first table of the law, that is, with those which required man to adore God alone.

In particular, Luther charged that, instead of calling upon the name of the Lord alone, and instead of "sanctifying" the name of God, religious invoked their own name, and "sanctified" the name of their order, and of their founder.

Nor would it do to say that this holiness of the religious state, of the order, and of the founder was simply a participation in the holiness of Christ. This distinction came, in Luther's opinion, as too much of an afterthought to acquit the monks of error here—the proof of which was, he thought, the so often repeated contention that the religious state was superior in holiness to the ordinary Christian one.

Furthermore, this idea of participation in the holiness of Christ seemed to Luther wholly unacceptable. "Christ alone," he repeatedly replied to such representations, "Christ alone is holy; and by no other name does he allow us to be sanctified and saved."

Confirmatory evidence of the monks' abandonment of the true worship of God was the way in which they celebrated the office in their churches. They attended rather to staging a performance, with strict attention to the rubrics, than to praising God with their hearts as well as with their lips, and to listening to his word.

The vows were equally opposed to the second table of the commandments of God, that is, those concerned with duties towards parents and towards one's fellow men. Obedience to parents was the specific object of a commandment, and service of one's fellow men was similarly required by God, while in contrast the vows were only institutions of men. Therefore, in order not to sin against God, when the vows came into conflict with duties of obedience to parents or aid to neighbor, one would have to refuse the vows any claim. Unfortunately, one found nothing of the sort: religious in fact took advantage of their vows to escape submission to their parents. Some, on the plea of their vows, went so far as to throw off all the bonds that united them to their families. Far from seeking to serve their fellow men, monks thought that the whole world ought to be at their service, since they themselves, they claimed, served God.

Luther criticized this point of view very violently, and set out to demolish the arguments which the monks brought forward on their side:

a) They claimed that since obedience was better than sacrifice, the service of one's fellow men would itself have to be placed under obedience to one's superiors. Luther answered that the Lord held in horror any sacrifice contrary to his own law of obedience to parents and service of neighbor. The vows, therefore, could not bind against the will of parents or the needs of others. Furthermore, he reminded his readers, obedience to parents and service of others—these were the service of God in the first place, and not the mumbling of prayers. The service of God conflicted with obedience to parents and service of others only when parents or one's neighbor called upon one to deny Christ: in that case one would have to obey God rather than men.

b) The monks would protest that it was better to obey one's spiritual parents than one's carnal parents. Luther replied that these putative spiritual fathers were fathers of error. Even the apostles, even the angels, would have to be disobeyed if they taught that it was good to break the commandment of obedience to parents and service of other men. And he added that in his opinion the idea that in spiritual matters man was free in relationship with parents and with others in general—this was an open door to all sorts of rebellion against the established order.

c) Finally, the monks claimed that they fulfilled their duty of fraternal charity and service inside the monastery itself. Conceding this point, for relations among monks within the same convent, Luther emphasized with all the more force that in relations between various monasteries and among different orders it was often hatred which was the keynote. Similarly, in the relations of monks with the needy there was no excess of love: monks were forbidden to leave the convent to aid the distressed.

5. The vows are opposed to reason.

It may appear somewhat astonishing that in a question of this kind Luther would bring into play so humanistic an argument. To counter this astonishment he was careful to explain at once that in this matter reason could have no positive, but only a negative, bearing. He explained that natural reason was incapable of saying what God is, but was capable of declaring, with great certainty, what he is not. Similarly, if it could not determine what is just and good in the eyes of God, it at least knew clearly what is not good, for whatever contradicts earthly truth does by that very fact contradict heavenly truth.

In this section there was to be little question save of the vow of chastity. Here more than in the preceding chapters Luther's intention seemed to be to show those who were chafing under monastic life that they were fully authorized by God to alter their career and take a wife. It was the irrevocability of the vow of chastity which seemed to Luther to go against reason. His fundamental rule in this question was the following: when a vow, even one blessed by God and valid in his sight, became impossible, it ceased to oblige, even in his sight. Thus someone who had vowed to make a pilgrimage but found it physically impossible to go was released from the obligation; and, similarly, someone who was imprisoned was unable to perform the duties of religious practice. So it was with the vow of chastity: from the moment that it became impossible, it ceased to oblige, and complete freedom to marry supervened.

Nor could it be said, he argued, that in the case of a divine commandment as in the case of a vow, it was the intention that counted, and not the exterior accomplishment. The object of the vow was, not the intention of preserving chastity, but real chastity itself, just as the object of any of the commandments of God was not the will to do such and such a thing, but the actual doing of it. The assumed counterarguments of the imaginary respondents to Luther's indictment, with their appeal to the sufficiency of intention were therefore insufficient. It must be said simply that in case of impossibility a divine commandment no longer obliged, and the same in the case of a vow of chastity which had become impossible: it had no further binding force.

Nor could it be said that the impossibility of preserving chastity (since the achievement was wholly interior) could not be likened to a case where the exterior activity required by a commandment became impossible of accomplishment. It was an error to believe that man could wrest dominion from the sexual force enthroned within him— a tyrant far more unapproachable than any exterior dictator.

For unaided man, doubtless, it was impossible to keep the commandments of God; but by faith this was made possible for him, and even easy. But in the case of the vows this aid was not given, for it was not God himself who willed the obligation of the vow. It was man who had imposed it upon himself; and he had no right to count on divine aid in the bearing of a burden he himself had shouldered. Consequently, the impossibility—where it existed—of preserving chastity was unrelieved, though it did not leave one with no resort but to break a divine commandment. It simply invited one to understand that a vow impossible to keep had no validity—and to act accordingly, that is, to marry.

Besides, Luther wondered, why should the situation created by the vow of chastity be something special? Why could not the same superiors who could dispense from different points of the very rule according to which the vows had been pronounced not also dispense from the vow of chastity in cases where it could manifestly not be kept? Here too it seemed contrary to reason that the vow of chastity should be excepted from the general laws of dispensations granted in the various religious orders.

The reasons given for this different treatment among different vows seemed to Luther insufficiently grounded. One basis was the eminent value of virginity, which, once lost, could never be restored; another was the moral importance, relatively, of chastity. The first basis, Luther insisted, was only consistent with the doctrine that placed works above faith, and therefore accredited a value to virginity for its own sake, and to perpetual chastity in itself. The second basis, said Luther, only indicated that the commandments were being measured, not by the majesty of the will of the God who had given them, but by a home-made scale of graver and lighter importance of matter. Luther utterly rejected, as alien to the Gospel, this distinction between graver matter and lighter matter; once an act became the object of a divine commandment, man was bound, without distinction of grave and not grave, to fulfil what God required.

3

6. Conclusion of the treatise.

In the final pages, which seem more polemical than the rest of the work, Luther marshaled a whole combination of arguments against the vows. With them he tried to show, on the one hand, that either the vows did not have as their object any obligations which were not incumbent upon all classes of men (and religious profession was therefore pointless), or else the vows did make some additional requirements which monks, however, did not or could not fulfil. On the other hand, he argued that the vow itself had nothing essentially irrevocable about it, since cases were provided for in which the vows —those of obedience and poverty, at any rate—would no longer have to be kept.

As for poverty, if poorness in spirit was meant by this, it was clear that it was not a "counsel" but a precept. As a consequence, choosing it by a vow came down to contempt for a commandment of the Lord and to a failure to take seriously the very promises made at baptism. If, contrariwise, material poverty was meant, this involved the loss of private ownership and disposability of material things, but not the loss of their use; yet it must be accompanied by a certain lack of food, clothing, and so forth. Now, as for material needs, monks scarcely suffered from them; rather, their houses were crammed with possessions of every kind. And was the vow irrevocable? Nothing of the sort. Let a monk become a bishop and he regained the right of property, and this, if you please, over the goods of the Church. One would be told, no doubt, that the episcopacy was such a state of perfection that it dispensed the vow of a monk consecrated bishop: this kind of argument Luther could not take seriously. No, seen in its true light, the vow of poverty had to be judged as a means for avoiding having to be bothered with the misfortunate and with the "real" poor, and to divert towards one's self the aid which should have been distributed to them.

The vow of obedience was open to similar dissection. If it meant evangelical, spiritual obedience, all Christians accepted it and pledged themselves to it by the very fact of their baptism. If it meant an additional obedience to a superior, in accordance with a rule, then strictly speaking it might be kept for a time, as a training process; but made the object of a definitive vow, it was in basic opposition with spiritual obedience. Nor was it wholly irrevocable, either; monks who became bishops were no longer bound to keep the vow; and superiors in a religious order were no longer obedient, but in command. As unacceptable in this case as in the case of poverty was the justification of the abandonment of the vow upon accession to the episcopacy on the grounds that this was a state of perfection. Besides, was it not the religious state that had been recognized by theologians as a "state of perfection"? For Luther, under this argument of accession to the episcopal state of perfection there was concealed the free choice by which monks could become bishops.

Superiors charged with command were dispensed from obedience; no doubt one would be told that they were the authorities desired by God. Luther recognized, of course, that in this post they could practice spiritual obedience—the kind common to all Christians—but not corporal obedience—the kind special to religious—not even, declared Luther, to other superiors. But it had been corporal obedience only which had been the subject matter of their vow. It was clear, then, that this vow of obedience, just like that of poverty, could be revoked. Neither the one nor the other, then, was a definitive and absolute vow; and ultimately, no one was bound, beyond mitigation or cancellation, by these vows.

To come now to chastity. A strict parallelism between it and the other two vows could not be established. At least one might say that there did exist a really evangelical chastity—voluntary chastity, freely preserved, clear of any obligation, practiced by certain people simply because it pleased them to live in that way, just as it pleased others to marry, or to follow this or that trade, or to make any similar choice. Vowed chastity, contrariwise, was not evangelical. To the many arguments which we have already had the opportunity to hear, Luther added this one: to make a vow of chastity was to make a vow concerning something which was not within our power. Even after a year of trial, we could not dispose in advance of our sexual instinct. Its intensity exposed us to the danger of some day finding ourselves in an impossible situation. Therefore, just as—in practice—the vows of obedience and poverty appeared to be revocable, so should the vow of chastity.

Only one obligation really bound us. In terms of it, all else besides was due to be judged. That obligation was love. Every commandment which did not bear an immediate reference to love could admit of dispensations and thus no longer bind human subjects. Such was the case with the vows.

After some rapid notes on the subject of widows, and especially on the text of 1 Tim 5:11–12, in which Luther could see no vow in the monastic sense of the term, he concluded briefly that monastic vows were to be condemned, and that those who had pronounced them not only could, but should, abandon monastic life.

As we have seen, the various criticisms that Luther thought fitting to bring to bear against monasticism in general, and the vows in particular, are quite numerous. But they are not of equal value. Some correspond with Luther's more profound intuitions, especially with his "rediscovery" of justification by faith; others are much more opportunistic, contentious, sometimes just skirting, or seeming to skirt, bad faith.

Apparently the most basic reason for Luther's rejection of the vows was his profoundest religious intuition, which, from his point of view, might be represented thus:

a) God only is holy, and is the only source of holiness.

b) This derived holiness exists only in and through Christ, who is thus the only way of reaching the fruit of holiness—salvation. Conversely, this is given to men through God's works achieved in Christ.

c) For his part, man must accept personally the salvation thus given, make it his own, or rather, be clothed with it. This he does through faith, and faith alone, solemnized in baptism. Baptism, on God's side the gift of salvation, is on man's side a pledging of himself to evangelical life—spiritual poverty, brotherly submission to all, etc., included.

The vows, it seemed to Luther, threatened this threefold intuition:

a) Monastic life implies a recognition of a source of holiness in creatures: religious life in general, particular orders, their founders, etc., the monks themselves becoming a source of holiness for others.

b) By establishing religious life, one had established a system of ways other than Christ for reaching salvation—that is, keeping the vows, keeping the rule, etc.

c) Religious life puts these works—of the vows and of the rule—in the place of faith, or above faith. Religious destroy evangelical liberty of conscience, which is not bound to any human work, and which produces as fruits of faith man's obedience to God's commandments. By the obligations born of the vows as adjuncts of faith, they pretend to create an elite, superior to ordinary Christians.

Doubtless one may find, in the other writings of Luther on monasticism or the vows, some other points of view, some other comments, some other judgments. In those writings, as in fact sometimes in the *De votis* here, Luther granted at least the theoretical possibility of an authentically evangelical monastic life, with really "free" vows— particularly as a means of education and formation of young people. Nevertheless it remains true that in the *De votis* as in the closely preceding *Themata de votis* Luther's rejection of monastic life and vows rests solidly on his major religious intuitions. In other words, Luther's attitude towards religious life, monasticism in especial, was not adventitious, secondary, and superficial; on the contrary, it was bound up with the very essence of his conception of the major truths of religion.

For Luther, in fact, the assertion of God's unique sanctity involves necessarily the denial of any participated sanctity. The affirmation of Christ as the only Savior of men involves the denial of any active participation on the part of any creature other than Christ in the salvation of the human race, and especially the denial of any active part played by any man in the accomplishment of his own personal salvation. Finally, the recognition of faith as the unique source of justification necessitates the rejection of works. All this concretely contributed to the constitution of Luther's fundamental intuitions.

However, Luther's negative conclusions do not so evidently follow from his positive assertions. It is precisely at this point that there is room for an effective criticism, from the Catholic point of view, of Luther's position on the vows.

Without going into detail—to do so would require another volume —we can at least say (aided by Father Bouyer's work, *Du Protestantisme à l'Eglise*[8]) that the clearest data of the New Testament dispute the validity of the negative conclusions supposedly deducible from Luther's positive affirmations. If God alone is holy, this does not mean, for the Bible, that his sanctity cannot be communicated to men; quite to the contrary. If Christ is the only Savior, this did not

---

8 L. Bouyer, *Du Protestantisme à l'Eglise*, coll. "Unam Sanctam," XXVII (Paris: Editions du Cerf, 1954).

prevent St. Paul himself from being able to help pay off, in his own flesh, "what is lacking in Christ's afflictions for the sake of his body, that is, the church."[9] If faith, finally, is the unique source of justification, none the less St. Paul cautioned the Philippians: "You must work to earn your salvation, in anxious fear."[10]

Thus Luther's attempted association between his positive affirmations (of a traditional character) and these negations or denials appear not to be of biblical, and certainly not of New Testament, origin. It is for this reason fundamentally that we cannot agree with Luther's assertion that a strict bond exists between his positive rediscoveries and his rejection of religious and monastic life.

If, however, Luther's fundamental intuitions formed, at least in the sixteenth century, the very basis of the Reform, it does seem that the rejection of monastic life and of the vows forms an integral part of that basis. We shall see this better when we have considered the position of a certain number of other Reformers.

---

9 Colossians 1:24.
10 Philippians 2:12.

Chapter II

CALVIN'S POSITION

It is not difficult to determine the different aspects of Luther's position on the vows and monastic life. The documents in which the German Reformer expressed himself on this subject are plentiful. With Calvin the case is somewhat different. Calvin, of course, had not known religious or monastic life through personal experience. A cleric he was, yet unlike Luther he did not receive ordination to the priesthood. We do not find in him, therefore, the personal interest which led Luther to become preoccupied so especially with monasticism.

Many people today know Calvin as the author of *The Institutes*. This work has been of very great importance ever since the Reformation. Many editions of it, often re-edited, appeared even during the lifetime of Calvin.

In the 1541 edition of the *Institutes*[1] Calvin devoted but one important passage to the religious life. Often the reader expects him to take up the matter, especially when he is handling the fundamental themes on the basis of which monasticism had been condemned by Luther. Thus in Chapter XIV,[2] on Christian liberty, Calvin asserts that the

> third part of Christian liberty directs us not to scruple about external things which in the eyes of God are indifferent and shows us that we can either do them or not do them, indifferently. And the knowledge of this liberty is very necessary to us. For, if we have it not, our con-

1 This edition of 1541 was published in 1936 by the society of Les Belles Lettres, under the patronage of the Guillaume Budé association.

2 Chapter XIV is to be found in Volume IV of the Guillaume Budé edition, pp. 129–147.

sciences will never find rest, and will be endlessly occupied with super-
stitions. In the judgment of many people today we are ill advised to
take up the discussion of whether we are free to eat meat, whether we
are free in our observance of feasts and fasts and the usage of vestments,
and of such trifles, as it seems to them . . .³

It is enough to have read a few pages of Luther on monasticism to
expect here, from the pen of the French Reformer, some application
—if only a word—of this idea of "Christian liberty" to the spiritual
problems posed by religious life. As a matter of fact we find nothing.

So it is with Chapter XV,⁴ "On Ecclesiastical Power," where Calvin's intention is to show that the councils, which Catholics suppose
to be immune from error, have turned out to produce some decrees

the impiety of which I might easily demonstrate by evident arguments,
were I not striving to be brief, as I must be in this treatise . . .⁵

Certain councils, for instance, had forbidden marriage, or the use of
meat, while according to St. Paul, in 1 Tim 4, this prohibition is
"hypocrisy and falsehood." From Luther this text would have drawn
almost infallibly a clear reference to monks, or to members of the
clergy, to whom the Church forbade marriage. But, here again, nothing of the sort: Calvin lets go by the opportunity to express, even by
so little as a word, some opinion or assertion on the vow of chastity
for religious or of celibacy for priests.

We may cite a quite brief reference in Chapter XIII,⁶ "On Five
Other Ceremonies Falsely Called Sacraments: To Wit, Confirmation,
Penance, Extreme Unction, Holy Orders, and Matrimony"; but to
tell the truth no very important conclusions can be drawn from it.
The subject is bishops, and their claim to be successors of the twelve
apostles and to rank above ordinary priests. Calvin agreed with those
who rejected a difference between bishops and priests, and he added:

The mendicants wish to be esteemed as representatives of the apostles,
wholly through a comparison, in which monks and apostles are quite
dissimilar: yet this is why they traipse here and there and live off others'
possessions. For the apostles did not run giddily from one place to
another, as do these vagabonds, but went wherever they were called by

3 *Op. cit.*, p. 135.
4 *Op. cit.*, IV, pp. 149–196.
5 *Op. cit.*, p. 175.
6 *Op. cit.*, IV, pp. 73–128.

God, to make the Gospel bear fruit. Nor did they lazily load their stomachs at others' tables; but in accordance with the liberty given them by God, they availed themselves of the kindness of those whom they instructed in the word. Nor need the monks cover themselves with borrowed feathers, as if there were no means of identifying them, seeing that their title is indicated well enough by St. Paul. "And now we are told," says he, "that there are those among you who live in idleness, neglecting their own business to mind other people's" [2 Th 3:11]. And in another place he says, "They count among their number the men that will make their way into house after house, captivating weak women whose consciences are burdened by sin; women swayed by shifting passions, who are for ever inquiring, yet never attain to recognition of the truth" [2 Tim 3:6-7]. Let them own to fitting these descriptions, and leave to others the office of the apostles, for they are worlds away from it.[7]

There is nothing in this passage which has in view monasticism itself. Calvin simply made his own the criticism expressed so often in his times (even by the most dutiful Catholics) against the wandering monks and friars of that day, busily tramping the fields in search of churches and religious houses off which to sponge. At any rate it may be concluded that Calvin rejected the comparison between the life of the apostles and that of these mendicants more, it seems, from esteem of the apostleship than from disesteem of the religious life.

In 1559 Calvin published the seventh and last edition in Latin of the *Institutes;* it was translated and published in French in 1560.[8] If we find few things on monastic life in the edition of 1541, we find in the fourth book of this last edition, in contrast, a veritable little treatise on the vows.

Already in Chapter VIII of Book II, Calvin had briefly rejected, in connection with his treatment of the ten commandments, the classical distinction between precepts and counsels. With the latter, Calvin wrote, scholastic theologians "declared that a choice exists either to comply or not to comply." Here the counsels in question, according to Calvin's conception of the matter, were those

commandments which our Lord had given as well to Jews as to Christians, on the subject of refraining from a desire for vengeance, and of loving our enemies.[9]

---

7 *Op. cit.*, pp. 104–105.
8 This edition was recently published by the Société Calviniste de France in Geneva (Labor et Fides publications).
9 *Op. cit.*, II, p. 177.

As a matter of fact, what were in question here were precepts of the law, observance of which was required of all Christians.

But it was in Book IV that Calvin devoted a whole chapter—the thirteenth—to the subject of the vows.[10] Here he treated of the vows in general first, and especially of their lawfulness. In his opinion, this lawfulness had to be judged according to three criteria:

a) The criterion of the promissee of the vow, the one to whom it is made. A vow is a promise made to God, and valueless unless what is promised is pleasing to the one to whom the promise is made. But God has explicitly revealed what is pleasing to him; therefore, no human contrivance, but only God's expressed desire, can fulfil the requirement of "pleasing God." Thus

> all the services which we have invented by ourselves to please God are not pleasing to him, whatever pleasure we may ourselves find in them. In point of fact, in several places in Scripture God not only rejects them but utterly abominates them.[11]

b) Criterion of the person who makes the vow. A vow is a promise of something which is within the power of the one who makes the promise—and would be otherwise meaningless. Besides, it must correspond to something the promisor is called upon to do by God, and must not curtail the benefit of the liberty which God himself has given to man. Thus from this point of view (which we may designate as the subjective one) the vow of celibacy is not admissible. For it consists of promising something which does not depend upon man himself, without a call from God to such a form of life, except in some temporary fashion. Moreover, it implies a certain contempt of man's God-given freedom to marry.

c) Criterion of the intention: Why make a vow? According to Calvin, the purposes which a vow may lawfully serve are four: as regards the past, to render thanks, or to do penance; as regards the future, to protect one's self against dangers, or to incite one's self to the performance of duties.

> We hold as good all vows which look to any one of these ends, especially vows concerning things external to ourselves, so long as they have God's approval as their support and are commensurate with the graces he has given us.[12]

10 *Op. cit.*, IV (Chap. XIII), pp. 242–265.
11 *Op. cit.*, p. 243.
12 *Op. cit.*, p. 248.

Measured by these criteria, the vow implicit in baptism is wholly legitimate—the more so since it is willed by God himself. As for particular vows, to judge them one must have recourse each time to the three criteria just stated. Moreover, Calvin advised that vows be used with caution, on account of the danger of superstition:

> How much superstition long reigned here is well known. One man would make a vow to drink no wine, as if this abstinence were in itself something pleasing to God; another would oblige himself to fast; still another, not to eat flesh meat on certain days which they fondly imagined to be endowed with more sanctity than others. Other vows were more childish still—though it was not children who made them. For it was taken for great wisdom to vow to go a-palmering hither and thither, afoot, or half dressed, so as to extract more merit from the fatigue.[13]

This groundwork being laid, Calvin went on to give the reasons why he rejected monastic vows and hence monasticism. Monks customarily justified their way of life by invoking the example of the primitive Church. Calvin was to answer this argument first. For him, the comparison between monks of, say, St. Augustine's time and sixteenth-century monasticism clearly showed the corruption this form of life had undergone.

Under the pretext of contemplative life, the monks, who in other days applied themselves assiduously to public and private prayer, to reading, and to study, had nowadays turned into lazy do-nothings:

> Those of our day repose the principal part of their sanctity in idleness. For take away their idleness, and what will become of the contemplative life whereby they think themselves more excelling than other people, and even deem themselves close to angels?[14]

Formerly monks had doubtless led a highly austere life, but in liberty and charity. Their sixteenth-century counterparts

> consider it almost an unforgivable crime if some one fall by the tiniest mite short in following their regulations in the matter of clothing, or of food, or of other frivolous observances.[15]

All this had its importance. But the weightiest item in the scales for Calvin was that the monks had reached the point of envisaging

13 *Op. cit.*, pp. 249–250.
14 *Op. cit.*, pp. 253–254.
15 *Op. cit.*, p. 253.

their way of life as a state of perfection. Supposing themselves to form an elite group, the monks imagined "that there was a way of life more perfect than that which Jesus Christ gave without distinction to his whole Church."[16]

Their state of perfection consisted, according to the monks, of having given up everything to follow Christ, and especially of having renounced, for him, all material possessions. But here, according to Calvin, was a fundamental error: placing perfection in something other than charity, and in such a way that charity itself was thereby compromised. By their state of perfection, and by the profession by which they entered this state and which they considered as a second baptism, the monks separated themselves from the Church; having a rule of behavior of their own, they wished to receive the sacraments separately from others, they cut themselves off from the fellowship of the faithful, and thus formed schismatic conventicles, or sects, each attached to some particular learned teacher, and hostile to one another.

All these criticisms were made by Calvin in contrasting the monastic state in his times with that in the days of the primitive Church:

> By this comparison with the monasticism of old, I feel I have done what I claimed I should do: to make plain how falsely our sanctimonious neighbors allege the example of the primitive Church in seeking cover and defense for their state; for it is clear that the monks of old were no less different from them than men are from monkeys.

These judgments, nevertheless, lead as if necessarily to a rejection of the very principle of monastic life, or at least to an extreme skepticism.

> It seems like a fine thing to give up all one's property so as to be free of every earthly care; but God is gladder rather to have a man, free of all avarice, ambition, and other fleshly desires, be charged with governing his family holily and well, having as his intention and purpose to serve God in a just and approved calling.
>
> It is a fine thing, or so it appears, for a man to retire from the company of his fellows and, aloof from the world, to pursue philosophy. But it is worlds removed from Christian love for any man, as if from hatred of humankind, to flee to some barren place and there to stay, alone, withholding himself from the very principal thing which our Lord requires of us all, and that is helping one another. Even should we concede that

16 *Op. cit.*, p. 255.

there is no other evil in this way of life, still it would be enough by itself that it has introduced into the Church a dangerous and noxious example.[17]

As for the monastic vows themselves, they are to be condemned, root and branch, for three reasons:

First, especially since it is their intention to invent a new service of God in their station, to please him, and to gain his grace, I must conclude, on the principles already stated, that all that they vow is naught but an abomination before the face of the Lord.

Secondly, since their dreamlike creation of a way of life has no regard for God's calling and looks to him for no approval, it is, I say, a rash boldness, and therefore unlawful.

Thirdly, since they are constrained to several modes of behavior which are perverse and wicked, as are the idolatries committed in all their convents, I say that therefore they consecrate themselves, not to God, but to the Devil.[18]

The vow of continence, moreover, should be rejected for two reasons: one, "that they falsely believe it a service pleasing to God"; the other, that it is "made rashly by those who have not the power to keep it." The other vows, obedience and poverty, Calvin rejects without further specification, on the general grounds he has already given; and he adds that they seem to be made "in order to jest at God and at men."

Thus the enforced conclusion: Monastic vows are unlawful and therefore do not bind in conscience; moreover, being abominable to God, they should be abrogated; God save us from remaining in them.

The *Institutes* of 1559 thus included, as we have just seen, a certain systematic teaching by Calvin on the monastic vows.

In other works (written before this last edition of the *Institutes*, however) we can find elements which were preparing little by little for the synthesis which we have just examined. A glance at some of these documents may be not without interest.

In the course of the years 1549–1550, the movement created by the Reform reached a critical point: The military successes of the German Catholics, the opening of the Council of Trent, internal divisions among the "protestants"—these boded ill for the future of the Reform. To restore courage and to strengthen the integrity of the

---

17 *Op. cit.*, p. 260.
18 *Op. cit.*, p. 260.

Reform, Calvin dealt with the contemporary stumbling blocks in his *Traité des scandales*, published in 1550.[19]

Among the stumbling blocks which threatened to cause many people to turn out of the path of the Reform, Calvin noted among others that of "those who live evilly, while professing to adhere to our doctrine." The dismal truth of the accusation Calvin by no means denied; quite to the contrary. But the question for him was whether having adhered to the Gospel—that is to say, in his language, to the Reform—had made men worse than they were before this "conversion." As a point of comparison, Calvin chose the reputedly greatest sanctity on the side of the adherents of the papacy, namely, the monks: "For if there is any sanctity on that side, the monks say that it is among them; and no one contradicts their assertion." But, he noted, "nowhere do we experience a stronger stench than thence." To Calvin's nose, in fact, monasticism was comparable to a wallow, to a barnyard; it was like Sodom; it was like, in a word, hell. Those who left it should occasion no astonishment if they led a still dissolute life:

> As for their being lazy bellies, mutinous, treacherous, disloyal, ungrateful, inhuman, addicted to piques and to cliques, slavish thieves, lechers—is there not a whiff here of the order and nature of the cloister? I know, of course, that each order of monks has its own rule, peculiar to itself; but this they have in common, that all are endowed with the splendid virtues I have just celebrated.

Furthermore, when a monk came over to the Reform, Calvin thought that he should be subjected to a long period of trial.

> Were I dispensing justice, and had I the means to enforce it, when a monk fell into my hands I should never let him go until I had examined him and knew him of my certain knowledge half a year or more, keeping him on trial. I should not want them to mix in society, for fear they might spoil others. At the end of the term all those that I detected were not really unfrocked in their hearts I should put to work underground like convicts or fence them in, in some park, like wild animals.[20]

For Calvin, it was thus clear that the monks, under an appearance of sanctity, had accumulated many more vices than one could find among members of "the Gospel." Without directly condemning here

---

19 The *Traité des scandales* was published in Volume II of the *Œuvres de Jean Calvin* (Je Sers and Labor publications, 1934), pp. 142–297.

20 *Op. cit.*, pp. 255–256.

monasticism itself, he strongly delineated its blemishes: in so doing, however, he was no more violent than many Catholic preachers of the sixteenth century.

And so, when Calvin repeats his accusation, some further pages along, that the monks are addicted to the pleasures of the table; when he says that those

> who preach on the austerity of the popish discipline provoke redoubled laughter, for who is there to believe this praise of their fasts and their abstinences from a monk with a bloated red face, and belly to match?[21]

and when he adds:

> I say that almost all the clergy on the papist side are like a swamp miasmatic with every stinking vice and wickedness, and not only sending its bad smell out on every side, but corrupting and infecting all the rest of the world with this deadly odor,[22]

his words do not differ essentially from the customary oratorical violence of his day.

It will be more interesting in view of our purpose to note, at the end of the treatise, the position expressed by Calvin on the subject of chastity. Three points are advanced by the Papists against the Evangelicals: the question of confession, the question of Friday abstinence, and the question of celibacy. On the last point,

> the Papists would make us think that all the disputes between us are like a war which we have stirred up over women.

Doubtless the context lent itself to impeachment of the monks' profligacies. Calvin was unsparing:

> Everyone knows that the cloisters, the cells, the holes of the monkeries smell of nothing but excrement. I stop at naming their greater secrets, for they are enormous. Yet why dissimulate what everyone recognizes as surely as if I had already said it? As for the monks, they do not deny that these fine fathers have leisure for frolicking. What shall I say of the priests who, far from being ashamed of their lechery, boast of being known as great whoremasters, flying as it were the banners thereof? . . . It is a shorter rein for a man to live in marriage with a wife than to keep papal continence, which consists in merry-making at every corner . . . It seems in fact that these fine fellows keep their beds

---

21 *Op. cit.*, p. 267.
22 *Ibid.*

empty of one wife just so that they may have freedom to invade all the beds of married folk; and, indeed, they do besmirch everything with their foul deeds. For they have a proverb among them, that priests and monks must provide for themselves wherever they can; and it is plain to see how they put it into practice, and how busy they are at that pursuit. And confession comes along as nicely for it as could be, since it is like having nets spread to catch all the poor women who are in any degree fragile. They do catch them, and moreover provide one another with them. [23]

At the same time, however, Calvin adds more deep-lying reasons for his rejection of perpetual chastity and of the vow binding to it. He bases his objections on the contention that since marriage has been instituted by God, men have no right to abolish it.

Marriage binds man and woman mutually, with an obligation that comes from God himself; no human authority, then, extends to freeing man and woman from their reciprocal obligation. "God created the human race in such a state that the man is head of the woman, and she his helpmate; and thus he bound them to each other." Before original sin, marriage remained only a divine gift and a blessing. "It is insufferable that men should abolish God's so great benefit." After the fall, in a world blemished by sin, marriage became also a remedy designed by God for the weakness of human flesh: "So that, to escape unchasteness, everyone will have his wife, and every wife her husband." This is the remedy offered to all who "cannot contain themselves"; and let there be no falling off in the application of this remedy, for it is one intended by God. "The prophets, apostles, and martyrs, indeed the great part of the most excelling and most holy personages who have ever lived, have used this privilege." [24]

While thus leaving, it seems, the at least theoretical possibility of celibacy, for those who can contain themselves, Calvin was here emphasizing the fact that marriage is not a spiritually undesirable state. He contradicts flatly the notion of the superiority of virginity and celibacy over marriage. He rebukes those who imply that an authentic Christian life is scarcely possible in the marriage state. "This madness has reached the pitch," he wrote, "of attaching the taint of infamy to marriage."

23 *Op. cit.*, pp. 275–279.
24 *Op. cit.*, p. 277.

We have here, then, some very clear elements of Calvin's doctrine concerning one aspect of monastic life: the vow of chastity. This, for him, was disdain for marriage, divine institution though it is, and for its dignity; it was a distortion of voluntary continence, to which certain people might be called, but which could never, even for them, become obligatory; and, finally, it was disobedience to the order intended by God.

In his *Commentary on the First Epistle to the Corinthians* in 1546, with a new edition ten years later,[25] Calvin confirmed these elements. In the "argument" preceding the commentary, Calvin clearly indicated what in his opinion was the direction taken by the reflections of the Apostle Paul in the seventh chapter of the epistle:

> The seventh contains a dispute touching virginity, marriage, and the state of continence called celibacy. As is to be presumed from what St. Paul says, among the Corinthians there had arisen a superstitious opinion that virginity was a surpassing, an almost angelic virtue (so that they held marriage in despite, as something profane). To dispel this error, he directed each individual to look to what had been given him, and not to venture here beyond his powers; for not all have the same calling. Thus he shows who may abstain and who may refrain from marriage, and to what end such abstinence must tend; and, on the other hand, who are bound to marry, and what the real rule of Christian marriage is.

In the commentary itself, on verses 32–34 of this chapter, Calvin explains first that, if St. Paul commends celibacy, it is because "he well knew how heavy are the burdens of marriage." And therefore "he who can remain free of it should not reject such an advantage." Among the disadvantages which marriage may entail (not of its nature, as Calvin takes care to point out, but because man has "violated the holy ordinances of God") the Reformer's list includes disillusionment ("Led to believe that they should find here nothing but sweetness, they are disappointed of their hopes"), disputes between husband and wife, material cares, and shortcomings of children. Besides, marriage entails solicitudes which may

> arise out of gaiety, for instance, all the foolishness of wedding parties, frivolous pastimes, and other such things with which married people are accustomed to occupy themselves.

---

25 *Commentaire du Nouveau Testament*, Paris: Librairie de Ch. Meyrueis et Compagnie, 1955; the *Commentaire sur la Première Epître aux Corinthiens* (dedicated "au Seigneur Galliaze Caraciole") is in Volume III.

4

Paul wishes Christians to be free from these discomforts and solicitudes, "so that they can direct all their thoughts and affections to the
Lord God." But Calvin notes that the process is not automatic: the
fact of being unmarried does not *ipso facto* produce single-minded
interest in the things of God.

> Yet he does not mean that those who are not married are always given
> over to God. For experience demonstrates the very opposite in priests,
> monks, and other religious, especially since nothing is more remote
> from God than their celibacy.

Calvin does not here give reasons for this last judgment. But some
lines further along he takes it up again and develops it, in connection
with verse 34, where St. Paul says that a woman free of wedlock is
intent on holiness, bodily and spiritual. Paul

> shows us what is true chastity, pleasing to God, namely, keeping one's
> conscience unsullied in his sight. And would to God that his had been
> better seen to than has been the case! As regards the body, we see in
> what way monks, other religious, and all that priestish excrement and
> clergy of the Pope have sanctified themselves to the Lord. For is there
> to be found anything more unspeakable and more vile-smelling than
> their celibacy? But now to leave aside the modesty of the body: How
> many are there not of them who enjoy the admiration of the people,
> on account of the public conception of their chastity, yet who burn
> within with monstrous concupiscences? Here we are prompted to recall
> the declaration of St. Paul that no chastity is pleasing to God save it be
> of mind as well as of body. I wish that those who warble so haughtily
> of continence would get it into their heads that they will have a different
> tune to sing with God. Then they would not be so bumptious and bold
> when they come up against us. Who among them dispute of this matter
> more pompously than the very ones who wanton publicly without the
> slightest shame. Yet though they conduct themselves as cleanly as they
> will before the eyes of men, yet all this is nothing if they do not also
> keep their minds intact and pure of every filth.

In other words, the celibacy of monks and priests does not correspond to that which St. Paul recommends to Christians, and would
wish for all, as permitting more leisure for the Lord. On the one
hand, monks and priests have little more than the appearance of
celibacy: they "wanton without the slightest shame"; on the other
hand they do not understand that in the matter of continence they
will "have to deal with God"; they do not preserve chastity pleasing
to God, "which is as well of the mind as of the body." The sign of

this is, for Calvin, their opposition to the doctrine he preaches himself, and against which they are "so bumptious and bold" as to debate.

Coming to verse 35, Calvin finally gives two principles in accordance with which he feels celibacy is to be validated; first of all:

> for what purpose celibacy must be desired; that is, not for its own sake, nor because it is a more perfect state, but to the end that there will be nothing to keep us from cleaving to God—which is a Christian's sole business all his life long.
> Secondly, no snare must be thrown over consciences by anyone's being forbidden to marry; for everyone must be allowed his liberty.

As for the latter condition, Calvin clearly emphasizes that it is not fulfilled by "those . . . far bolder than St. Paul, who have not boggled at forbidding marriage for clerics," nor by those who have made vows "of perpetual continence, which are snares whereby so many millions of souls have been dragged down to everlasting perdition." For Calvin, then, celibacy is a praiseworthy thing, recommended by the Apostle, when it is envisaged as something to make one more wholly at God's disposition, without any idea of the superiority of the state of celibacy over that of marriage, and on condition that the single live in liberty, that is, without a vow.

This last point enables us to give a very clear account of Calvin's position as to the vows in general, on the basis of what is said here explicitly of the vow of perpetual continence: they are opposed to spiritual liberty, the liberty which the Holy Spirit guarantees to Christians. To make perpetual vows or recommend that others make them is to rebel against the Holy Spirit, because to do so binds "conscience in a matter in which he wished them to remain free." Unless, Calvin adds ironically,

> the Holy Spirit since then [the times of the Apostle Paul] has changed his mind, and now requires, that is, a snare which he formerly disapproved of.

Commenting on verse 37, Calvin repeats that to make vows is to condemn one's self to perpetual slavery; the "resolution" and "deliberation" required of the father of a family in making up his mind to give his daughter in marriage or to keep her in the single state—these are not comparable to the monks', which are "voluntary fetters of perpetual servitude."

Nevertheless, he proposes to himself an objection: Must the vows be condemned if they are made in such a way that the following conditions are present: firm and deliberate purpose, and actual ability to carry them out in accordance with the ordinance of God? To this objection Calvin answers only as regards the vow of chastity: one cannot know with certainty whether the gift of continence is permanent:

> We are uncertain of God's will for the future. Let us use the gift for the space of time it is lent us; yet let us commend ourselves to God, and be ready to follow wherever he calls.

We see now why Calvin rejects the vows, that of chastity in particular: they bear on the future, that uncertain future which is never in the hands of men, but ever in the hands of God, or, better, spread sail-like to the breath of the Spirit, of which nothing in the life or department of Christians must restrict the liberty. We do not undertake here to criticize this argument, based on a somewhat anthropomorphic conception of God and of the Holy Spirit, as well as of divine liberty in relationship with the decisions of man. We merely note that it is one of the arguments most frequently brought against the obligation of the vows, and against religious life.

From Geneva, in the month of June, 1548, Calvin addressed to "the Right Noble and Truly Christian Prince Edward, Duke of Somerset, Count of Hertford, etc., Protector of England and Ireland, and Royal Guardian," his *Commentary on the First Epistle to Timothy*.[26] In Chapter V, on verses 9–13, he once more has occasion to allude to the question of the vows, and most especially to the vow of continence. Here, in these verses, St. Paul envisages the employment of certain women in the service of the Church, and he indicates the conditions thereof. May there not be here a certain form of vows recommended by St. Paul himself?

The first thing to be noted, Calvin declared, is that the widows whom St. Paul recommends receiving into the service of the Church must be at least sixty years old. How did it come about that this prudence on the part of the Apostle failed to inspire the discipline of the Papists?

> Now if the Holy Spirit proclaimed by the mouth of St. Paul that no women are worthy of being admitted to this office [service of the Church]

---

26 *Commentaire du Nouveau Testament*, Vol. IV.

unless they are over sixty, since it is dangerous to live outside marriage below that age, then what pride and temerity it has been to have since imposed a law on girls in the flower and greatest warmth of youth bidding them abstain perpetually from marriage! St. Paul, I say, does not admit abstinence from marriage, unless in mortified old age, well beyond the danger of incontinence. Later, forty was the age settled upon for the consecration of virgins to religion (so called), and then afterwards thirty. Finally, no attention was paid to age at all, and they were received indifferently, young and old together. . . . What folly, what cruelty, thus to throw a rope around girls still quite young, for whom marriage would be so much more fitting.

The result of this premature admission to the service of the Church was, as St. Paul had forseen, "frolicking at the expense of Christ." Adds Calvin:

Pray you, how many monstrous and horrible sins are the daily spawn of compulsory celibacy of religious in the Papacy? What cloisters, bars, or grills could be placed there and restrain the carnal appetite? And even supposing that things had at first gone well, still, after so many and such terrible experiences, they should have changed their minds and submitted to the advice of St. Paul. But quite to the contrary, far from doing so, more and more from day to day they provoke God's anger by their obstinacy. But not alone of these religious do I speak: they compel priests and monks as well to abstain from marriage their whole lives long. Yet within them there boil unnamable lusts, so that scarce one in ten of them behaves chastely. And when it comes to the monasteries, plain fornication is the least of all that goes on there. Would their ears open but once to God speaking through the mouth of St. Paul, how they would leap to the remedy which he ordains here; but such is their pride that they turn like tigers on those that would help them to it.

Thus we recognize here certain criticisms from the *Commentary on the First Epistle to the Corinthians*. Briefly, monks, priests, and other religious do not preserve the chastity or celibacy which they vow.

Papists wish to see in verse 12 the justification of the vow: widows unfaithful to their engagement in the service of the Church are reproved by Paul for "incurring the guilt of breaking the promise they have made." For Calvin, this is a "witless argument." For, even if in fact widows were led to contract their services to the Church, nothing can be concluded from this concerning the vows, first because the end in view was not that sought by those who now make vows, and then because these widows were of a much greater age than that at which in Popery girls are permitted to make these vows.

First of all, the end is to be considered. The reason why widows formerly promised not to marry was, not to be able to say that they then led
a holier life than they would have led in marriage, but because they could
not be dedicated at the same time to the service of their husbands and to
the service of the Church. But in Popery a vow of continence is made as
if it were in itself a virtue pleasing to God. Moreover, in those days they
renounced their freedom to marry at an age no longer suited to marriage.
For they had to be at least sixty; and by having been content all this time
with one husband they gave ample warrant of their chastity. But nowadays among Papists vows to renounce marriage are made before or in
the midst of the flower and warmth of youth.

And it is here that Calvin gives the two basic reasons why he rejects the practice of the vows, at least if we extend what he says here
of the vow of perpetual continence to all those which form the
foundation of the religious life.

We disapprove of this tyrannical law of perpetual abstinence from
marriage for two reasons. The first is that they are imagined to be a service meritorious in the eyes of God; the second, that they hurl poor souls
down to ruin through the rashness of vowing lightly and without careful
forethought.

The two causes cited by Calvin for rejection of the vows are here
clearly expressed: on one hand, the idea of merit attached to the vows
and to the religious life of which they are the basis; on the other
hand, the rashness of a premature commitment. And it does seem
that here the Reformer accepts the idea of a commitment such as
widows might make, under the conditions laid down by St. Paul:

They did not make directly a vow of continence, as if the marriage
state were barely pleasing to God; but only in so far as was required by
the office to which they were being deputed did they promise for the rest
of their lives not to contract the bonds of marriage. And so for their de-
priving themselves of the freedom to marry, they did this at an age when,
had they continued as free as could be, it would still have been unfitting
and unsuitable for them to marry.

Otherwise put, this commitment by widows was acceptable because it had in view directly the service of the Church, for which the
widows renounced marriage without disesteeming it, and furthermore because in point of fact their very situation moved them not to
marry; thus by their commitment and its consequences of definitive continence, these widows were in all truth doing nothing but
what their years prompted them to do anyway.

Here we conclude our citation of evidence of Calvin's attitudes. Doubtless many other writings might be consulted. Yet we feel that in the collection of texts presented is to be found the essence of Calvin's doctrine on the vows. Calvin rejected the vows, and consequently monastic or religious life: we feel this is a clear deduction, whatever nuances remain to be supplied.

He did so first of all for practical reasons: convents and monasteries were not places where life was lived chastely; quite to the contrary. Furthermore, to the promise of the vows was adjoined, among monks and religious, the idea that their state in life was meritorious, and from this point of view superior to the marriage state, so that the general tendency among them was to look down on the divine institution of marriage. If celibacy had a certain superiority over marriage, it was purely practical: celibacy permitted a greater freedom, at least material, for the things of God. Finally, the promises made by religious were generally entered into much too lightheartedly: the very age at which commitment through vows was officially permitted was anything but a guarantee of well-founded choice and mature deliberation. Aside from these practical reasons, Calvin rejected the vows more fundamentally on theoretical grounds:

a) Marriage is a divine institution, obliging in principle, which binds man and woman mutually; it is at once a blessing from God and a remedy for human weakness, preventing disorders of the flesh.

b) Man must obey God and remain ever ready to answer any divine call: hence, he has no right to bind himself by a commitment which mortgages the future instead yielding its free and entire disposition to the Holy Spirit.

c) The vows create a state of servitude, opposed to the spiritual liberty of a Christian, in matters which God has left open to human choice.

We do not intend to set forth here in detail the manner in which the arguments brought forward by Calvin might be answered from the Catholic point of view. His practical criticisms could, to tell the truth, in large part at least, be accepted. In religious houses in the sixteenth century, abuses (though they were not so general as one might believe from reading Calvin and other authors—even Catholic) were numerous. That a certain scorn of life "in the world" came to birth in these religious houses, and even in certain theological texts of the time—such, too, is the testimony of history. And, finally, that quite often, too, commitments had been made without sufficient maturity is equally certain. Here again, let us repeat, these regrettable facts must not be generalized a priori; and numerous specific reforms —for example, among the Hermits of St. Augustine—had attempted, sometimes with success, to put a halt to the abuses described.

Calvin's theoretical criticisms seem to us unacceptable from the Catholic point of view because, in our opinion, they are founded on a certain number of confusions: Christian marriage is understood in some degree as a necessity of nature, the liberty of the Holy Spirit is identified practically with a certain form of highhandedness, and Christian liberty is confused with something that comes closer to caprice and to fancy than to real liberation from one's self and from sin.

That marriage is of divine institution no one will deny. But in the New Testament it is quite clear that marriage is not the only vocation possible, as we shall be better able to see in the third part of the present volume. For another form of service has been proposed by God himself, and it, too, is blessing from him. Doubtless it involves risks; yet it does not lead necessarily—quite to the contrary—to disorders of the flesh.

If that vocation is possible according to the New Testament, the fact implies that the response which a man called thereto may make to it is by no means in disharmony with personal disposability to God. This disposability does not consist in following arbitrary directions, call these the liberty of the Holy Spirit or not, as you please, but in conforming one's self to a certain stable "order," willed by God himself, and analogous to the commandment of the Father which it was Christ's calling to fulfil.

As will be better seen in the later pages of this volume, it is the idea of "vocation" which enables us to explain the "commitment" of religious, and to show that this commitment does not suppress a Christian's spiritual liberty, but, contrariwise, fulfils it.

Chapter III

OTHER REFORMERS

WE have seen Luther's position on monastic life, which he himself had lived for several years. Calvin was less interested than his German predecessor in monastic life and the vows; however, in his writings, too, we have been able to discern the major lines of a judgment on this institution of the traditional Church.

We must give the other Reformers, or at least some of them, a rapid glance. As is well known, the sixteenth-century Reform movement was sustained by numerous pioneers in the various countries of Europe in that day. Those pioneers left behind them a very abundant literature. To review this today, in full detail, would be wearisome; at any rate, we feel it will suffice to take some samplings of it here and there.

We had the opportunity earlier of seeing the influence of Karlstadt and of Melanchthon on the formation of Luther's thought on the vows. We recall that their criticisms bore especially upon the vow of chastity.

We shall see later the influence of Melanchthon in the editing of the text of the Augsburg Confession—the expression, in 1530, of the faith of Luther's disciples. After the Diet of Augsburg, this Augsburg Confession became the object of a refutation from the Catholic side. To bring the issues to focus, Melanchthon, on the Lutheran side, was charged with writing an *Apologia* for the Confession.[1] Herein, when dealing with monasticism, Melanchthon presented the criticisms,

---

1 The text of this *Apologia* is to be found in *Die Bekenntnisschriften der evangelisch-lutherischen Kirche* (Göttingen: Vandenhoek and Ruprecht, 1955), I, pp. 139–404 (see pp. 377–396 for Article XXVII, on the monastic vows).

47

now familiar to us, customarily advanced on the Reformation side, and attempted to show that the biblical texts usually cited by the monks and their defenders were not in fact applicable to the "flight from the world," nor to the poverty, obedience, and chastity, assertedly achieved in the monasteries. So it was with the classic pericope (Mt 19:27–29), and especially the conclusion: "And every man that has forsaken home or brothers, or sisters, or father, or mother, or wife, or children, or lands for my sake, shall receive his reward a hundredfold, and obtain everlasting life." This promise, commented Melanchthon, does not apply to those who, "with no calling, without God's order," leave all that they have; it is addressed solely to the persecuted:

> The subject here is that other abandonment, executed by God's order, when for example a tyrannical power seeks to compel us to deny the Gospel; for then we have God's order to undergo rather any loss, and to see snatched from us not only riches, and wife, and children, but even life. This is the abandonment that Christ recommends to us here, and that is why he specifies: "For the sake of the Gospel" (Mk 10:29).

Melanchthon makes a similarly oriented commentary on Christ's call (Mt 19:21) of the rich young man: "If thou hast a mind to be perfect, go home and sell all that belongs to thee; give it to the poor, and so the treasure thou hast shall be in heaven; then come back and follow me." Evangelical poverty, Melanchthon explains,

> does not consist in the abandonment of possessions, but it consists in not being avaricious, and in not putting confidence in riches like David, for example, who was poor at the very height of power and riches.

The position of Zwingli (1484–1531), the Zurich reformer who, as is well known, was opposed at once by Lutherans, Calvinists, and Catholics, may be glimpsed in the perusal of some of the sixty-seven theses which set forth his teaching and make up the treatise *Auslegung und Gründe der Schlussreden*[2] of 1523. Thus, Thesis XXVII rejects even the possibility of religious orders, on the score of the universal brotherhood of Christians:

> All Christians are brothers, and know no man on earth as their father; and thus the religious orders collapse, and the sects, and separatist groups.

---

2 Cf. the article "Zwingli" (by Cristiani) in *Dictionnaire de théologie catholique*, XV, ii, 3716–3744, and "Zwinglianisme" (by J. V. M. Pollet), *ibid.*, XV, ii, 3745–3928.

Thesis XXVIII opposes the vow of chastity:

Everything which God allows either is not forbidden, or is good; and therefore marriage is proper for all men.

Similarly, Thesis XXX:

Those who make a vow of chastity have a silly and childish confidence in themselves, which proves that those who require such vows of others are guilty of shameful conduct towards pious men.

Thesis XXXIII is aimed at religious poverty:

Property now given unrightly to temples, convents, monks, and nuns ought to be distributed to the needy, unless it is restored to its legal owner.

Even a rapid reading of these theses brings once more in view the criticisms habitual among the Reformers. The religious state is contrary to the one means of holiness (which is, to use Zwingli's terms, to live in sonship in relationship with our only Father, who is in heaven) by setting up founders of orders as sources of holiness, and in creating among members of the same order a brotherhood different from that which all Christians have in common among one another. The religious state, founded on the vows, involves a disdain for the order of creation, in which marriage is the normal situation of man and woman. More basically, the religious state rests upon man's confidence in himself, and on the idea of merit, and of the remission of sins and justification through the performance of human works.

All this we have already considered several times, and there is no need to dally over it.

More original, it seems, was the position of Bucer (1491–1551). We find it given expression in the last work of the Strasbourg reformer, written in 1550 during his exile in England, upon the request of Archbishop Cranmer. With the purpose of establishing a truly evangelical regime in England, Bucer composed his *De regno Christi*[3] as his life's chief work, gathering together there the whole of his doctrine.

---

3 The *De regno Christi* is in Volume XV and XV *bis* of the edition *Martini Buceri opera latina* published by Les Presses Universitaires de France and by C. Bertelsmann Verlag. Volume XV contains the Latin text established by F. Wendel, and Volume XV *bis* the French translation of 1558, also established by F. Wendel.

True, he does not treat in it explicitly of the vows nor of religious life. But he explains at length his notions about marriage—notions, by the way, which place him in opposition to the greater part of other reformers on a number of points (for example, on the question of divorce). Among the thirty-two chapters which Bucer devotes to marriage, out of the seventy-five which make up the total of *De regno Christi*, there are three which concern the vow of continence and are, therefore, of pertinent interest to us here.

In Chapter XXIII[4] we find explained "How marriage was permitted by the Sainted Fathers even after a vow of perpetual continence." Using citations from St. Cyprian, St. Augustine, and Pope Gelasius, Bucer seeks to establish that forbidding marriage to those who have made a vow of perpetual continence is not in conformity with the teaching of St. Paul, nor with at least a part of patristic tradition:

> Forbidding these widows to marry after a vow of continence is a noose slipped over them whereby they may find themselves falling into fornication.

In fact, he adds, and this time not basing himself upon patristic authorities:

> they offended much more grievously when they rashly took that vow of continence, than when they then placed the word of God ahead of that vow, recognizing their infirmity,

which is to say, when they broke their promise, by reason of their weakness, in accordance with St. Paul's direction: "But if they have not the gift of continence, let them marry; better to marry than to feel the heat of passion."[5]

Treatment of the vow of continence afforded Bucer an opportunity to state a fundamental principle for all the vows:

> It does not accord with reason that a vow made by men should be preferred to a principle given us by God, and to what the Holy Spirit has told us is preferable.

Consequently, Christians are not bound to keep all the vows they have made, "though they be made in view of something praiseworthy and holy." In this whole question, the essential thing is to have the call:

---

4 *Op. cit.*, XV *bis*, p. 165 ff.
5 1 Cor 7: 9.

We may not undertake, we may not impose upon ourselves, any obligation, however holy and worthy it may be, if we have not been called upon to do so by God.

Must it be concluded from this that no vow must be made, since none is called for by God? It does not seem that this conclusion corresponds exactly to Bucer's thought, at least in Chapter XXIII. Indeed rather, it seems from the context that Bucer touches here very rapidly upon something which was to be developed much later, especially by the brothers of the Protestant religious communities of the twentieth century: justification of a definitive commitment by a divine *vocation*. At any rate, however, Bucer does point out the basic reason why certain people may "preserve continence": the gift of God.

It is certain that when God calls us to some vocation, he provides for us, furnishing us with those of his gifts and graces which are necessary for it.

It is the same idea of a particular call which is picked up in Chapter XLV:

Those there are who have been definitely created for marriage by God; whoever forbids them to marry, for any reason whatsoever, is going against what has been ordained by God.[6]

According to Bucer, in fact, the gift of continence is not to be likened to the gifts "necessary for all persons, for their salvation." He puts it, instead, in the category of gifts

which are destined for and promised to some specific individuals, and consequently are useful for them, like the gifts of various kinds of knowledge, and various tongues, and endowments of mind, of body, and of external possessions.

Of course, the gift of continence is necessary "for young people," or again for those who find themselves, though married, in some circumstance which prevents them from living conjugally.

To these God will not refuse the gift of continence, if they ask it of him by pure and holy prayers, and lend their own efforts to possessing it and keeping it.

But those who are of an age for marriage and not prevented from living conjugally must not "disdain" the marriage state and ask for

6 *Op. cit.*. XV *bis*, p. 22 ff.

themselves instead the gift of continence: they will not obtain it. Only those can obtain it who have received from God this special vocation of continence either "for a space of time" or "for life."

God, in fact,

appoints . . . for all his children a certain vocation and way of life, conducts them, and puts them to good use when the time is right. He makes clear also the position and condition in which it pleases him that each should exist, and by what means each may fittingly honor and serve . . .

Thus God picks out certain ones to whom

he gives the gift of making themselves eunuchs for the Kingdom of Heaven—to some for the whole of their lives, to others for a certain time only.

So, it is a matter of vocation. But the question arises how to recognize this vocation. To tell the truth, this problem did not seem to embarrass Bucer greatly. It would be enough to rely on God through humble prayers and thus obtain a firm assurance of one's vocation. Anyway, in the last analysis it is the conscience of each individual which has to be the judge: no power, neither secular nor even ecclesiastical, has the right to any determination at all in the matter. And the judgment of conscience as to vocation to marriage or celibacy is also final.

We may discern here the fact that Bucer's position on recognition of vocation not only renders unacceptable the obligation of celibacy for clergy and monks, but also excludes any possibility of a religious community, in the strict sense of the term. Extending the question, in fact, to the subject of the vows, one may say with assurance that if Bucer recognized that certain individuals may be called by God to live in obedience, poverty, and celibacy, for a limited time or even for life, there would be no other obligation upon them than that dictated by their own consciences, to the exclusion of any social interference, including that of a hypothetical religious community to which they might some day attach themselves. For there would be no stability possible in such a community, no authority, nor, finally, in fact, any pooling of personal possessions, since each individual would always be able to appeal from the community to his own conscience, and thus put his property to his own use, or act outside of— or even in opposition to—the established authority.

So, then, if Bucer recognized the validity of celibacy for someone who had received a vocation for it from God, he none the less rejected vows of celibacy, or even stable and definitive commitments received by any power other than an individual's own conscience. In the following chapter, in which Bucer examines "the words of the Holy Spirit written in the first to the Corinthians, seventh chapter, touching the praises of continence," nothing new is added to the foregoing save a more violent criticism of obligatory celibacy of the clergy on the side of the papacy. To remedy numerous evils, these "unhappy fruits of a state of continence observed without the vocation from God . . .," it would be very useful,

> nay, altogether necessary, not to forbid to anybody, whosoever he be, for any reason, nor on grounds of any forfeit, the honorable state of holy marriage.

Chapter IV

PROFESSIONS OF FAITH

As the result of the foregoing rapid survey, the position of the Reformers on monastic life and the vows must be fairly clear to us. While maintaining the theoretical possibility of a religious (that is, monastic) life, the Reformers were opposed to the idea of a definitive and "sacred" commitment to a form of life which did not seem to them definitely founded on the requirements or regulations of the Gospel.

Without any doubt, the judgment they passed on the monastic and religious system left its mark on Protestantism: the disciples of Luther and Calvin persisted more strongly in the condemnation of this form of life than details of this or that document now suggest. Nevertheless, the judgments of Luther, Calvin, and other Reformers on the religious life had nothing normative about them: they were simply the ideas of those who expressed them; they were respected because their authors were respected as great religious thinkers but, properly speaking, they were not binding upon the Churches which resulted from the Reform.

Not exactly the same thing is true of the official texts in which these Churches gave express formulation to their profession (or "confession") of faith. Though it is true that these documents do not have an absolutely normative and definitive force—in contrast, for example, with the "canons" of ecumenical councils in the Catholic Church—still, they do much more than express one particular view of the Christian mystery. The Churches, in these documents, profess ("confess") their faith; and by virtue of this profession they extend thereto, not, to speak precisely, their "authority"—this would be to attribute to them a Catholic conception of the visible Church—but their "mission" and their "response" to the word of God.

The Augsburg Confession

AFTER some years of hesitation, Emperor Charles V, as will be re-called, convoked the Diet of Augsburg, to meet in the summer of 1530 in order to search out means whereby an entente might be established between Catholics and the disciples of Luther. Theologians on both sides set to work. On the basis of a "confession of faith" drafted by Luther himself as an appendix to his treatise on the Last Supper, *Vom Abendmahl Christi*, the theologians of Wittenberg, Melanchthon being first among them, established a text approved by Luther in May, 1530, and, after several rehandlings, read June 25, 1530, at the Augsburg convocation. If the purposes of Charles V were not accomplished—the entente between Catholics and Lutherans not having been reached—at least the various positions of the latter were officially determined, on both dogmatic and practical questions.

That text, known ever since as the Augsburg Confession (*Confessio Augustana*), was the Lutherans' first confessional document properly speaking. In it, one chapter is devoted to monastic vows; and it is for this reason that the Augsburg Confession interests us here.

Of course, this part (Chapter XXVII) of the Augsburg Confession contains no surprises for us after what we have read of the declarations of Luther and his disciples. But the conclusion reached by this document is clear and decisive: "Monastic vows are null and void; they bind no one." The arguments leading to this conclusion are taken for the most part from Reformation writings of before 1530.

"In St. Augustine's time, the monastic state was a free one." This declaration of Luther's, historically false, was the point of departure for the Augsburg Confession treatment of the vows. They had been invented, therefore, only after the relaxation of discipline and doctrine,

for the purpose of re-establishing discipline by means of the prison, so to speak, thus contrived. In addition there were invented, besides these monastic vows, other shackles and burdens with which to laden people even before they had attained the age of reason.

5

The first objection advanced against the vows was, therefore, that they had no historical reason for being except as restraints upon liberty, especially that of young "monks" or young "virgins" untimely inducted into the monasteries, or of people enticed thither by advantage's being taken of their ignorance about the validity of monastic life. It was therefore necessary, to counter this abuse, and to counter the means used to leave monks in their error, "to make heard and understood . . . the nature and aim of what we preach and teach."

In the second place, the Augsburg Confession directs attention to the fact that according to the Catholic conception the vows cannot oblige when taken contrary to papal law; then "a fortiori neither could they oblige against, and prevail against, the law of God." This went especially for the vow of chastity. "All those who are not made for single life are at liberty, and have the right, to marry," and this in conformity both with the commandment of God and with

the order of nature, established since the creation, which constrains, obliges, and impels into marriage all who have not received from God the special gift of virginity.

On the subject of this same vow, it was to be recalled besides that no commitment could oblige in case of impossibility; it was not even valid if it was not entirely the business of the person who took it, or if it was not taken in complete liberty.

But it is well known how little it lies in the power of man to live in a state of perpetual chastity. Besides, there are few men and women who have made their monastic vows on their own initiative, with full consent, and after mature reflection.

Even were it valid despite the lack of liberty or of discretion, this vow would still not entail the dissolution of a marraige contracted later; it was the authority of St. Augustine himself that was invoked in defense of this viewpoint.

The Augsburg Confession went on to more fundamental and, it might be said, more objective, reasons for the rejection of the vows, namely, that the vows implied the idea of justification through men's works.

St. Paul . . . everywhere teaches that we must not look to obtain justice through systems of conduct and of worship invented by men, but that justice and holiness valid in the sight of God come from faith and confidence, we believing that God accepts us into his grace for love of Christ, his only son. Now it is a fact that the monks teach and preach that their false spirituality has the power to satisfy for sin and to obtain the grace of God and justice. What do they thereby, if not to diminish the glory and preciousness of the grace of Christ and to deny the justice of faith? The conclusion must be that such vows have constituted impious and false worship. That is why they are null and void.

Null and void; but worse still, they caused to fall from the grace of God those who sought to be justified by them, and brought a whole series of errors in their wake; the monks went on to claim that their merits could be communicated to other persons; they supposed theirs to be "the perfect state," and thus led other Christians to look down upon the marriage state, private property, and so forth.

Through having heard monastic life falsely boasted about, simple folk end up by conceiving all sorts of dangerous ideas. Thus, hearing celibacy exalted beyond all bounds, they are troubled in conscience over the fact that they themselves are married. Similarly, upon being told that only mendicants are perfect, they cannot understand how ownership and profit can be sinless.

The Augsburg Confession concludes this matter: "Such are the numerous errors and impious notions entailed by the monastic vows." And it sums up:

They would render man just and holy in the sight of God, they would constitute Christian perfection, they would fulfil both the commandments and the counsels of the Gospel, they would embrace works of supererogation for which one would not be beholden to God. Granted now that all this is mere invention, falsehood, and emptiness, the monastic vows are null and void, and they oblige no one.[1]

In the Smalkald Articles,[2] written in 1537 by Luther himself, we find the pure and simple rejection of these vows:

Since the monastic vows are directly opposed to the first article, they must be abrogated .... He who vows to live in a monastery believes that he will lead a life better than that of other Christians, and that by his works he will merit heaven not only for himself but also for others. What is this but denying Christ? Worse still, out of their St. Thomas they conclude that the monastic vows have the same value as baptism. This is blasphemy against God.[3]

1 Cf. *Die Bekenntnisschriften der evangelisch-lutherischen Kirche*, I, pp. 31–137 (on Article XXVII, see pp. 110–119).
2 *Ibid.*, pp. 405–468.
3 *Ibid.*, p. 461.

Reformed-Church Confessions

THE Augsburg Confession and other Lutheran documents are quite explicit on the subject of monastic life and the vows. The various professions of faith of the Reformed ("Calvinist") Churches are customarily much less so. Many such confessional texts make no mention of the subject, and others only brief allusion to it. Thus, the La Rochelle Confession,[4] definitively established by the 1571 synod at La Rochelle, but already adopted in its first form at the first synod of the French Reformed Church in 1559 in Paris, contains a brief, though explicit, rejection of monastic vows. Article XXIV, in fact, rejects all man-contrived means of assuring redemption, since it is Christ who is our sole mediator, and he alone who saves us. The vows, as elsewhere pilgrimages, indulgences, and other things besides, are condemned for two reasons: these contrivances of men, being purely human inventions, do not derive in any way from the word of God; and they are attempts to substitute man's activity for God's, effected through Christ for the salvation of mankind.

> Finally, we hold purgatory to be a sham out of the old shop, from the same shelves as monastic vows, pilgrimages, forbidding of marriage and the use of meat, and the ceremonious observances of days—by all which grace and salvation are thought to be merited, and which we reject, not only for the false worth of merit attached to them, but also for being nothing but human fabrications which impose a yoke on consciences.[5]

The profession of faith known as the *Confessio helvetica posterior*, published in 1568 at Zurich,[6] is somewhat less laconic on the subject of monks, vows, and religious celibacy. In Chapter XVIII, which treats of ministers of the Church, one paragraph is devoted to monks.[7] Monks and orders, we read here, were instituted neither by Christ nor by the apostles; to top that, they are of no good to the Church; quite to the contrary, they do it harm. However, it must be

---

4 *La Confession de foi des Eglises réformées en France*, called the La Rochelle Confession, in modern French with notes and biblical references, *La Revue réformée*, No. 10, 1952/3. The 1559 text was published in *Bekenntnisschriften und Kirchenordnungen der nach Gottes Wort reformierten Kirche* by the Evangelischer Verlag, Zolliken-Zurich, 1938, pp. 65–79. The English translation here is based on the citation of this critical text in the French edition of the present volume.

5 *Ibid.*, p. 71.

6 Cf. *Bekenntnisschriften und Kirchenordungen*, pp. 219–275.

7 *Ibid.*, p. 254.

admitted that in times past monks might be tolerated: they were then true "monks," that is, solitaries, who worked with their hands to fill their needs instead of being a charge on other Christians, as sixteenth-century monks are; and, finally, like all good Christians, the monks of old submitted to their lawful pastors. But now they are no longer tolerable, despite the appearance of holiness they give themselves with their vows; in fact, they lead a life contrary to the promises they have made. "In our Churches," the paragraph concludes, "we have none such, and teach that there should be none such in Christ's Church."

Chapter XXIX treats of marriage and the family; it devotes several lines also to celibacy.

> Those to whom God has given the gift of celibacy, in such a way that they can continue wholly pure in heart and mind without grievously burning, must serve the Lord in this vocation as long as they feel endowed and protected with this heavenly gift, and so long as they do not therefore raise themselves up above other people, but assiduously serve the Lord in all simplicity and humility. Moreover, such individuals are better disposed to busy themselves with things divine than those who suffer the distractions of their families. But let this gift be afterwards taken away from them, so that they undergo a constant burning and sting, then they must remember the words of the Apostle, that it is better to marry than to burn.[8]

Evidently, the *Confessio helvetica posterior* admits, then, of the possibility of a celibacy consecrated to the service of the Lord. But this form of service is not definitive; the gift of celibacy is understood as a temporary one, which God can revoke. Consequently, there cannot, on the strength of this gift, be any commitment on the receiver's part to the service of the Lord: there is no place for a vow.

---

8 *Ibid.*, p. 273.

CONCLUSION

FROM the foregoing inquiry, in one sense unduly rapid, and yet already rather long, on the attitude of the Reform towards monastic vows, we can, it seems, draw some very clear conclusions.

On the whole, the Reform rejected monasticism as non-evangelical. It did so for concrete reasons: the state of religious houses was such, the abuses there so numerous and grave, the lack of fervor so manifest, the absence of authentic vocation so general, that the only solution possible seemed to them to be to suppress the religious houses and to liberate monks and nuns from their vows, especially the vow of chastity.

But at a deeper level the Reform judged the very principle of monasticism unacceptable. The basic reason for this rejection was that because of the monastic vows Christians were divided, according to the Reformers, into two categories: on the one hand, the *ordinary Christians*, who followed the *precepts* of Christ in "normal" human life, including professional activity and a family life based on marriage; on the other hand, *elite Christians*, who thanks to their "religious profession" embraced a state of perfection, defined by the addition to life of the *evangelical counsels*. Ordinary Christians—select Christians; precepts—evangelical counsels; marriage—celibacy; the Reform refused this whole division, would not agree that celibacy was of higher value than marriage, and opposed the idea that the evangelical counsels raised up in the Church a superior class of Christians to whom the counsels were reserved. Why this attitude?

To tell the truth, this rejection was related to the reillumination cast by the Reform on one of the fundamental principles of Christianity: justification by faith.[1] It was that principle which, in the eyes of the reformers, destroyed fundamentally the basic *raison d'être* of monasticism. Not man's works made man just in God's sight, but faith. Consequently, the justice that man has does not depend upon works which he can perform; whatever the difficulty or heroism, and whether matter of precepts or counsels, these human works leave him in the position of a sinner at enmity with God. The justification of man depends solely on the work of Christ, with whom a Christian's connection is *faith;* and from this basic standpoint monks and "ordinary Christians" are on equal footing. There is no place for "elite Christians."

No distinction between the two categories of Christians could be made save on the basis of works, considered as a source of human merit. That there were necessary works—as fruits of faith—the Reform (whatever has been said or written about it) maintained as a certainty: the Lord left us precepts to which we have no choice about submitting. They are necessary—not, to speak precisely, to gain justice or salvation, but as acts of obedience to the Lord. But in situations where the Lord has given no directions or precepts, where he has allowed each individual full freedom, no obligation can be founded upon obedience to the Lord. To make such works necessary is to ignore Christ himself. And it is to rely upon one's own merits as means necessary to salvation.

And that is another aspect of the Reform's rejection of monastic life. The vows constituted a kind of life in which the liberty of a Christian was disdained. For the Reformers, a Christian was doubly free. Fundamentally he was free in that his justice was not connected with the works which he accomplished himself, but only with the operations of Christ, to which faith gave man access. Secondarily a Christian was free in that Christ had given but one precept, that of charity, which freed a Christian from legalistic observances. In contrast, the monk made himself doubly a slave of his works: on the one hand, he found in his own activity the source of a supposed superior sanctity; on the other hand, he obligated himself to a large

---

1 On this reillumination of certain traditional principles, see Bouyer, *Du Protestantisme à l'Eglise.*

number of observances, of purely human invention, and more legalistic than the Law of Moses.

A Catholic critic may doubtless show that, in this chain of reasoning leading from justification by faith alone to the rejection of the
very principle of monastic life, there are a certain number of flaws.
The affirmation of justification by faith, for example, will not seem
to him to lead by unassailably logical steps to the denial of the merits
of a justified Christian in the performance of works. Similarly, the
affirmation of a Christian's liberty as regards the Law will not seem
to him to lead necessarily to the consequence of a condemnation of
commitment to some determined form of life recognized by faith
itself as a divine calling.

Thus to challenge these undue conclusions of the Reformers seems
to us necessary. In our opinion, it will be the pioneers of the renaissance of common religious life in contemporary Protestantism who
will be best able to furnish here the most useful elements of a con-
structive critique; and it is to their reflections, then, that we shall
appeal in the last part of this volume.

For the moment, the important thing has been to get a clear pic-
ture of the position of the Reformers: They rejected monasticism in
virtue of their "rediscovery" of justification by faith. In other words,
their rejection of religious life was dependent on their fundamental
principle—a principle, however, which Father Bouyer has shown to
have been perfectly traditional in the Catholic Church.

This rejection, however, left two doors timidly open:

According to Luther, Calvin, and others, there would be a place
in the reformed Church, in accordance with the word of God, for
"communities" aiming to educate pastors. In these communities
there might be found some kinds of "permanent" members, whose
"employment" would be to train and instruct pastors, as is done in
agriculture and crafts. But this was on condition that their way of
life should not separate them from the generality of other Christians,
or put ideas of superiority into their heads. Certain texts of Luther are
explicit in this matter, though few in number. Some "confessional"
texts also admit, though somewhat timidly, this same possibility.
Thus we read in the Wittenberg Articles of 1536 the following lines:

> If certain men of outstanding character, capable of living a life under
> a rule, feel a desire to pass their lives in the cloister, we do not wish to

forbid them, so long at least as their doctrine and worship remain pure, and, notably, so long as they consider the practices of monastic life as things indifferent. We are persuaded that numerous authentic Christians of irreproachable spirituality have passed their lives in convents.

It is even certainly to be wished that such convents will exist, occupied by wise and fervent religious, in which the study of Christian doctrine can be pursued, for the greater good of the Church. These might be then a place where, by the practice of pious exercises of religious life, young people would receive not only an intellectual training, but a spiritual one as well.[2]

On the other hand, certain Reformers, Bucer in particular, recognized more or less clearly the possibility of a divine call—temporary or even quite permanent—to a way of life other than marriage. In their eyes, it was possible that some individuals might be called by God to a life of celibacy. This *vocation* seemed to them to justify the renouncement of married life, though they considered marriage, as a general rule, required by God of man and woman. Doubtless this call to celibacy struck them as something entirely exceptional and phenomenal; doubtless, too, they rejected, as a response to this call, even the possibility of some commitment on the part of the individual concerned, and would not hear of the rights of any "community" in connection with this commitment. The fact remains, however, that the principle of a vocation to celibacy in the service of God was recognized by some Reformers. In the third part of this present volume will be seen how this idea has been developed by the members of twentieth-century Protestant religious communities. But first, in the second part of the book, we must be permitted to see some concrete realizations of community life in the Protestant world.

---

2 Cf. "Wittenberger Artikel, 1536," in *Quellenschriften zur Geschichte des Protestantismus*, 2. Heft, Leipzig, 1905.

Part Two

TRIAL COMMUNITIES AND MONASTIC RENAISSANCE

THE position of the Reformers, as presented throughout the preceding pages, was not a merely theoretical one. In fact, the Reform brought about the almost total disappearance of monastic and religious life in its midst. "Almost" but not absolutely total—for certain religious houses englobed by the Reform continued to exist, some of them even for a long time. Furthermore, some fresh attempts at religious community life made their appearance from time to time in the Protestant world, for example in the current of seventeenth-century Pietism, and again in the nineteenth-century deaconess movement.

But these different actualizations of religious community life were only trial establishments, involving nothing comparable to the monastic revival in our own day, as witnessed by the Darmstadt community, and perhaps more especially by the Taizé community. Nevertheless, we believe that a glance at the forerunners of contemporary Protestant religious establishments will be not totally devoid of interest; afterwards we shall see some of the present-day manifestations of the cenobitic revival.

Chapter I

MONASTIC SURVIVALS, AND NON-CENOBITIC TRIAL COMMUNITIES

The Möllenbeck Monastery[1]

IT is doubtless fairly difficult to know exactly how many monasteries were able to hold out after passing within the ambit of the Reform. What is certain is that this did happen despite the force of the Reformation tide. One instance of this somewhat astonishing situation was the monastery of Möllenbeck, situated near Rinteln, beside

---

1 Möllenbeck. Cf. *Quatember*, II (1954-1955), pp. 159-160.

the Weser. Founded in the ninth century, this monastery seems to have known days of greatness, particularly by virtue of literary activity there. In 1441 the house became part of the Augustinian congregation of Windsheim.

For reasons unknown, the Reform found a favourable echo in this monastery. For example, we note that around the year 1540 a Father Held (priest of the nearby village of Eisbergen), though he had become a Lutheran, continued to have none the less excellent relations with the convent. He came there quite often, and his sermons were received there with attention and esteem.

But it was not until 1558 that, under the direction of their prior, Father Hermann Wenig, the whole monastery transferred their allegiance to the Reform. None of the religious refused to undergo this "conversion," and none of them withdrew from the group as a consequence of it.

Despite this acceptance of the Reform, the routine of the monks remained essentially unchanged. Monastic regulations, the various ceremonies, choral chanting of the office—even Solemn Mass—went right on. In other words, the "conversion" did not show—except at the really sensitive points: the theology taught at the convent was modified in accordance with the new dogma, anything in the liturgy suggestive of the cult of saints was suppressed, along with anything (like processions) suggestive of the gaining of indulgences; and everything involving any idea of a sacrifice was withdrawn from the Mass.

In the spirit of Luther (which, as we have seen, left room for this role of the monasteries), a school was set up here from which a number of eminent minds were to receive their education. Many pastors in the area received at the convent an appropriate theological training.

If the monastery had few novices in the years preceding its reform, and exercised only a moderate influence in its area, after its reform it became, in contrast, very powerfully influential. The prior of the convent was besieged for advice by callers of every stripe. The number of novices, most of them natives of that area, increased quite appreciably.

Among the celebrated members of this convent, Conrad Hoyer is to be singled out for mention. In 1623, he published a sort of *apologia* for monastic life among Evangelicals.

Unfortunately, this monastery could not hold out against the troubles of the Thirty Years War. Despite the efforts of Hoyer to preserve the establishment, the crisis proved fatal. In 1675, the last "monk" of Möllenbeck died. Thus despite the unmistakable vigor of the monasticism here and its attempt at self-preservation, conditions in the Protestant ambient proved overwhelming.

Available information on this monastery and the life led there provides too inadequate a basis for sound judgment of it as an institution. But it is interesting to note that the monastic arrangement at the convent persisted after the Reform: the monks continued to live in obedience to their prior, to hold all their possessions in common, and to live a life of chastity. Did they keep the practice of the "vows" besides? Did novices entering the convent after its reform make a religious profession such as the older members there had made when they entered, pledging themselves in a definitive fashion to live in obedience, poverty, and chastity? We do not know.

Nor do we know anything more of other convents which passed into the Reform sphere. We know only that, generally speaking, they opened "monastic" schools in accordance with Luther's requirements.

The Herrnhut Community

IT is our good fortune to know a good deal more about the experiments in community living which grew out of Pietism.

Since they are often cited as forebears of present-day communities living under rule, we must say some word about them, devoting particular attention to the community of Herrnhut, near Zinzendorf.

Count Nikolaus Ludwig von Zinzendorf (1700–1760)[2] was possessed of a mystifying personality, at once strongly attractive and somewhat disconcerting. His most striking feature was a very lively sentimental attachment to Christ, not devoid of naive and childish elements, and, for Christ's sake, an inexhaustible devotedness towards all victims of persecution. In an era of intolerance, he was a passionate (if not altogether discerning) advocate of tolerance. In

2 On Zinzendorf and the Herrnhut community, see F. Bovet, *Le Comte de Zinzendorf*, Paris: Librairie française et etrangère, 1865.

face of the mutually violent opposition among religious bodies of the day, Zinzendorf was one of the first to seek for unity, insisting above all on the common religious experience of those who profess faith in Jesus Christ. In the latest biography of Zinzendorf in French, Felix Bovet's, he is considered a saint, with no doubt of his having lived in "experiential" intimacy with God. But it must be added that we are often put off by a kind of uncritical "illuminism" not without danger to the conduct of various affairs the management of which fell to his lot during his career.

If he had many adversaries (as well among Lutherans as among Calvinists, and especially among persons of influence), it must be confessed that this was not always without his having left himself open to accusation; but it was always—and herein is his greatness— through his having been faithful to his conscience and to his own convictions.

But this is not the place for a biography, however brief. If Zinzendorf interests us here, it is because of the community of which he was the soul: the Moravian Brethren of Herrnhut (Bohemian Brethren).

This "community" owed its origin primarily to the quite clear intention of Zinzendorf to provide a refuge on his lands in Lusatia for every Christian who might seek asylum there. But it also stemmed from the "reawakening" of Moravian Christians under the influence of Christian David's preaching and of the persecutions they were undergoing in their own country. In 1722 the first Moravian brothers arrived on the Zinzendorf land, and a first cabin was constructed at the foot of a mountain named Hutberg ("Protection Mountain"). This was their first house intrusted to the protection of the Lord: Herrnhut.

Herrnhut developed very rapidly; many newcomers arrived from Bohemia and agreed to become members of this "community." An association of several of Zinzendorf's friends (Shaeffer, Watteville, and Pastor Rothe) provided a guiding spirit for the movement. The members of this association proposed as their purpose to combat the kingdom of darkness and to extend the Kingdom of God. The means they sought to employ were the preaching of the Gospel "in spirit and in power," the institution of schools for the Christian education of children, the publication and distribution of books, and finally, contacts with Christians in other countries through correspondence and travel. It was in fact Zinzendorf himself above all whose career gave implementation to this last point.

In the daily expanding community of Herrnhut there was no lack of difficulties. The tension which offered most resistance was that created by the difference of religious bodies represented by the arrivals: some were Lutherans, others Calvinists, and still others of the Moravian denomination. Some members believed that all should accept the Moravian belief, others that every man should continue in his own. On the other hand, the brethren of the Moravian belief wished that in this new community, Zinzendorf, though himself a Lutheran, reinstitute the prior constitution of the Moravian Church.

But it was not until after several years of reflection and toil that this constitution was proposed by Zinzendorf and adopted by Herrnhut May 12, 1727.

The maintenance of this constitution was intrusted to a group of twelve elders, chosen by the community itself. The number of the elders, however, in the years which followed, was shortly reduced to four, and then to two, one of whom fulfilled alone the duties of guardian of statutes, the other being simply a deputy. The elders met for all decisions concerning the community; they decided nothing, however, without having first reached a common consciousness of the presence of the Lord. And this once reached, if the decision still seemed too difficult, or contrary opinions irreconcilable, they made a direct appeal to the Lord by drawing lots, in imitation of the manner in which the apostles, gathered together in the Cenacle, before Pentecost, had provided for the replacement of Judas by Matthias.

Members of the community were obliged to help one another in their spiritual life. To serve this end there was instituted the system of "bands"—little groups of two, three, or four members who gathered to confess their sins to one another, aid one another, and pray together. Frequent change of the makeup of the bands served to prevent the divisiveness which the system might have created.

On another, concurrent plan, the Herrnhut community was also divided into "choirs" in accordance with the various situations of the various members: thus there was a choir for the married men, another for young men of the brethren, another for little boys, and others for widows, married women, maidens, and little girls. Each choir was encouraged and directed by "workers."

Moreover, the brethren set up a court to administer justice whenever there was need, without its being necessary to refer matters to courts outside the community. Separate provisions were made for distribution of alms, the care of the sick, and the organization of work. All this emanated from the community and functioned through the active participation of members designated by the community. Everything was kept in control by "inspectors," who, when there was need, turned over to "censors" the charge of reproving those who failed in their duty.

Clearly, Herrnhut was set up as a fraternal city, with no occasion to appeal to anyone outside the community. For every need, there was a corresponding agency of the community itself to take care of it.

Every morning the community had to meet for common worship, held early, before time for tasks to be taken up. In the evening, the day ended with a gathering for the singing of hymns, after which the "word of order" was given and commented upon by Zinzendorf himself. The brethren of the community also met for "feasts of fraternal love," most often designated by the name of agapes.

Each "choir" also had its particular meetings, for prayer, reflection, and meditation on the Bible. In addition, the brethren kept "night watch": taking turns, they insured a "watch before the Lord," in expectation (quite biblical indeed) of the Lord's return. Finally, prayer had to be uninterrupted at Herrnhut. The brethren distributed the twenty-four hours of the day among themselves, each taking an hour of prayer and solitude.

The Lord's Supper seems not to have been celebrated very often. Several years after the formation of the community a more precise direction on the subject appeared from Zinzendorf: the Supper should be celebrated once a month. Later still, this celebration was prefaced by a symbolic practice in memory of the action of the Lord: the washing of feet.

Also every month, a special day was kept for prayer and thanksgiving.

In the matter of clothing there were specific rules only for women, the colors varying according to the different choirs. In any case, every superfluity of dress was prohibited, any ornament or jewel forbidden.

The dress of the men also had to be very simple: ordinarily brown or grey.

Outside times of prayer and meditation, the brethren of the community devoted themselves to work of various kinds. Of course, the organization of their employment was no easy thing; there were new-comers to be dealt with who, under the influence of a very fervent religiosity, were in danger of succumbing to the charms of the contemplative life, and, as the next step, to idleness.

The principal occupation seems to have been the cultivation of the Zinzendorf lands; this seems to have produced excellent results, for the community quickly became fairly prosperous. Work was not to be esteemed a mere servile necessity. According to Zinzendorf,

> witnesses of the Gospel are more strictly bound than others to work, so as not to be a burden upon anyone, and to be able in addition to give to those in need. To find employment for members of a commune or parish, whatever their trade, in a season of drought [Zinzendorf seems to speak from experience], amidst the difficulties which the malevolence of the world creates, besides the continual care that souls demand; to contrive that they shall always have work—this is one of the finest and most important tasks to be fulfilled by those to whom God has deigned to give any authority or post. They do not sin in busying themselves beforehand to provide for all this; on the contrary, they would sin in neglecting this duty.[3]

Besides the work at Herrnhut, certain brothers set out by twos or threes to bear witness to the Gospel. Sometimes they had a particular goal; at other times, impelled simply by the desire to do something for the Lord, they asked the community to call down the blessing of God upon their "message"; this was the name given at Herrnhut to this type of journey.

Though the intended hearers of these messages were a rather wide variety of sorts, it is interesting to note that the brethren sought to reach both civil authorities (for example, in 1727, Prince Charles of Denmark) and theologians at outstanding universities (Jena, Halle, Wittenberg, and others). Though well known, the fact still should be emphasized that the community was soon engaging in missionary activity abroad; Zinzendorf himself made a number of "missionary" journeys, especially during the whole of the time of his exile outside the territory of the Elector of Saxony.

---

3 Bovet, p. 129.

Doubtless the history of the Moravian Brethren of Herrnhut, and that of analogous foundations—at Herrnhag, in Holland, and in more distant places—would not be without interest. That of Zinzendorf himself, and of his eventful existence in company with his inseparable "Church of the pilgrims" (soon to become the directive cell of all communities attached to Herrnhut) is immeasurably rich. But it does not seem to be our business here.

We are concerned, instead, to draw conclusions from what has been already said here of Herrnhut. Beyond any doubt, we have met in it a "community" of Christians for whom the life of the first Christian community at Jerusalem was the ideal to be imitated and indeed realized anew (it, of course, has been the basic pattern for nearly all the cenobitical movements in the history of the Church). The objective of these people living on Count Zinzendorf's lands, and of the Count himself in gathering together these exiles and giving them a "constitution," was to revive in their own era the most authentic Christian life in history—that of the very first "Church" at Jerusalem.[4] At Herrnhut, members were "sedulously devoted to the teachings of the Apostles": every day they listened to, or studied, the word of God, meditated upon it, then made a still deeper study of it under the direction of Zinzendorf or of his immediate assistants; they were faithful to fraternal communion, gathered for meals in common, and met daily for prayer.

Moreover, Herrnhut beyond doubt was distinguished by outstanding spiritual fervor. The whole of the constitution was designed for the development of personal piety or—to speak more accurately— of personal religious experience.

But it is perhaps precisely for this reason that this "community"— everything considered—does not seem to us qualified for consideration as part of what may be called "Protestant monasticism." For this basic and thoroughgoing individualism makes the word "community," in its true sense, hardly applicable to Herrnhut, since individualism excludes common ownership of all things for the common good. Rather, though members did combine efforts in their prayers and their piety, this was for the improvement of each individually. It seems to us finally quite significant that one of the words Zinzendorf himself used to use when speaking of Herrnhut was

4 Acts 3: 42–47.

"sect." And that seems to be the right term, so long as its denotation does not extend to a sense of exclusion of all "outsiders."

More exactly still, we must speak of Herrnhut as a "city": a number of families, preserving their individuality, and their own property, were united in regard to a certain number of common activities, mostly in the sphere of worship and pious exercises; but the members of this "city" did not go beyond this level of commonage. In this connection, it is of the greatest importance to note the respect accorded in the community to the property of each member: material goods were simply not held in common. Each individual remained finally the lord and master of his own possessions. The "community" organization of Herrnhut may be similarly qualified: if there was obligatory obedience there, it was that of citizens to their city rather than that of monks in a monastery or religious in a convent.

For these reasons, then, it does not seem to us possible to count Herrnhut among the examples of religious common life in the realm of Protestantism—nor even to see in this (more "socialist" than "communist") city the ancestor of present-day Protestant religious communities. But at any rate we can credit it with an aspiration towards the concrete realization—in a certain form of community— of evangelical life and pursuit of things divine. On this score there is no doubt that Herrnhut (though it may surprise a Christian of the twentieth century, somewhat out of touch with pietism), offers testimony which we may accept with interest and gratitude, especially for throwing light on "parish communities."

In the pietist stream, however, there were still other experiments. Unfortunately, we have little exact information about them. We may mention specifically, at any rate, the community of the "Pilgerhütte," founded under the influence of Tersteegen (1697–1769). This community, more clearly "monastic" than that of the Moravian Brethren, was established on the property of a friend of Tersteegen's named Otterbeck. Here a group of fewer than ten companions were admitted so that they might lead a life in common, featuring especially prayer, meditation, and labor in silence. Tersteegen himself gave them what he called an "instruction"—somewhat different, it should be pointed out, from a rule in the monastic sense of the term—in which he insisted above all on prayer, religious experience, service, and peace. This community, very dear to the heart of Tersteegen, nevertheless turned out to cause him considerable pain: the spiritual fervor and religious emotion that developed there were not what he had looked for, nor what he himself sought to achieve in his own life. It seems, nevertheless, that this foundation was a strongly built one, for traces of it are believed to be found up until the nineteenth century.

Deaconess Communities

EIGHTEENTH-CENTURY Protestantism, as we have seen, was not devoid of feeling for religious community life: various experiments were undertaken to create "communities" within the Church. Now in the nineteenth century this desire for religious common life in Continental Protestantism was to take new forms.

By an interesting coincidence, these experiments (some of them successful) in Protestant religious community life were born at almost the same moment in France, in Switzerland, and in Germany—without there being, so far as anyone knows, any connection (in the beginning) among the pioneers of these separated movements.

In Germany, it was in 1836 that in Kaiserwerth, a little Rhenish village some miles north of Düsseldorf, Pastor Theodore Fliedner founded the very first community of Deaconesses. These sisters, as we may call them, were gathered here to render various public services: a shelter for the poor, an infirmary, and schools. But this foundation was also a response to a desire to revive in the Lutheran Church the ancient office of deaconesses; and it therefore considered itself a real "community" at the service of the Church.

According to the constitution of this first foundation and of the numerous communities of deaconesses which were then to be founded in the same spirit and to make up the Kaiserwerth Alliance, the sisters formed "a community of faith, of service, and of life." In view of this dedication the sisters, considering "their office as being received from God," understood themselves to be pledged to it for life, and especially understood celibacy as "a requirement of their vocation"; they received from their community everything that they had to have, and handed over to the community anything they might receive from the outside. And, finally, they submitted simply to decisions made by the community authorities. This common life for Church service involved, then, on the part of those who pledged themselves to it for life, the three elements of celibacy, common ownership of property (poverty), and obedience.

In Switzerland, in 1841, in his parish of Echallens, Pastor Louis Germond set up an institution not unlike Fliedner's at Kaiserwerth, and frankly designed to create "the Lutheran counterpart of the Catholic Sisters of Charity."

But it is the French foundation[5] of Pastor A. Vermeil and Mlle. Malvesin which strikes us as most interesting and deserving of a more detailed description here.

Pastor Antoine Vermeil (1799–1864) had first been involved in the Protestant "awakening" of the Church in Geneva around 1820. Pastor at Bordeaux from 1824 to 1840, he was then called to Paris, where an "awakening" similar to the one at Geneva was taking place around 1830, centering particularly around the Taitbout chapel. In 1840, the innumerable enterprises to which the "awakening" had given birth threatened to end with every one going his own way, if not in outright dissension. Pastor Lagny wrote:

> Just at that time our Churches were . . . sadly torn by party spirit and destructive individualism; often enough, love of self carried the day over renouncement of self for the sake of the Lord's work.

In this hour of danger, what was the reaction of Pastor Vermeil?

> To recover the deep and living unity of the Church—the Body of Christ —and the spirit of humility, prayer, and service which it supposes, there was required, he thought, something else than undertaking a variety of Christian activities, something else than institutions for the training of pastors, something else than ecclesiastical bureaus of coordination or central control. What was called for were souls entirely consecrated to their Lord, detached from themselves, and at God's disposition—souls whose solitary ambition would be to live completely by the Gospel, putting it into practice in the sight of men, and to preach by example and activity rather than by word.
>
> Our pastor was aware that there and then people were to be found in the Church who were attracted to this fundamental vocation—obscurely, perhaps, but none the less strongly—yet could not, because of the absence of any practical opportunity—answer the call.
>
> And so it was that, soon after he arrived in Paris, Pastor Vermeil resolved to work for the restoration in our Churches of "the religious orders of women" (the expression was his own). This would be, he ex-

5 On the deaconess communities, see G. Lagny, *Le Réveil de 1830 à Paris et les origines des diaconesses de Reuilly*, Paris: Association des Diaconesses, 1958.

plained, not some supplementary development in our Churches, nor
even something we were free to have or not to have, but the restoration
of a vital element then lacking in the Church's internal equilibrium, in its
vigor, and in its power to influence. We all know the zeal and per-
severance with which from that moment on he set out to realize what he
had envisioned.[6]

He disclosed his project to a certain number of women organized
as the "Lazarists" for the relief of reformed female prisoners. He
found that his project was in fact exactly what several members of
this group had been looking for. The need for "Protestant Sisters of
Charity" seems to have been felt in many quarters at that particular
time. But a still more definite step towards the foundation of a
community was taken when Pastor Vermeil approached, on this
subject, a woman who had been one of his former parishioners at
Bordeaux, and who was personally eager for a life consecrated to the
service of God. This was Mlle. Malvesin, to whom (February 6, 1841)
he wrote:

> For many years now I have entertained this idea of reviving—under
> another name, and without the superstitions with which they are
> tainted—religious orders of women to care for children, the sick, and
> old people.[7]

On this same day Mlle. Malvesin had written to Pastor Vermeil,
to place herself at his disposition:

> let this be anywhere at all, and the task never so humble, just so that it
> is really in the genuine service of the Lord.[8]

In the busy months which followed, definite decisions were quickly
reached by the two founders of the Deaconesses—the name they
agreed upon as emphasizing the primary ideal of service. The new
foundation was to be deeply conscious of its orientation towards the
coming Kingdom of God, and to be in fact a kind of sign of the
approach of this Kingdom. Members of this community were to be
devoted without reserve to their task of service; their disposibility
was to be given definite form through a lifelong commitment, to include obedience and celibacy; property was to be held in common;

---

6 Lagny, pp. 42–43.
7 Lagny, p. 46.
8 Lagny, p. 51.

there was to be a sister superior to direct the community "with authority," and, above her, the Rule, the authority of which was to be sovereign.

The spirit of this community was to be above all a spirit of charity, which was to take the form of manifold services to fill the shocking needs—and there were many of them—of the age. Interiorly, the deaconesses' whole life was to be oriented towards the development of the authentic spirit of Christ. And of especial importance for the age was the foundress's design to serve the spirit of unity among Christians by means of this community:

> Any undertaking where the spirit of a coterie appears, or of a faction, or of a sect, or of a party other than the great party of Christ—such an undertaking chills my zeal, freezes my powers of action.

And to these words—written February 10, 1841—she added:

> As for me, I know that my work will be to act, through the Lord, in such a way as to hasten the time when there shall be but one fold, and one Shepherd.[9]

It is also important to emphasize that, quite clearly, the two founders envisaged a project which would be wholly "evangelical"— by which they understood a project integrated into the Christian tradition which began with the Reform. Nothing could be clearer than their intention to operate wholly within the Protestant communions of France, both in the Lutheran and in the Calvinist line.

The Lazarist group received, in the house they had acquired at Reuilly, their first magdalen on November 6, 1841. A few months later, April 24, 1842, the community of deaconesses of Reuilly was formally inaugurated: there were at that time some five or six sisters under Mlle. Malvesin as sister superior. Their first task was to care for the repented women who came, and then, soon thereafter, to begin to visit the families of the neighborhood in which they were established.

The size of the community increased rather quickly. In 1845, three years after the official opening, there were eighteen sisters. Thirty years later, there were about fifty; and at the beginning of the twentieth century they numbered about seventy. Today, there are nearly a hundred.

The life of the community is chiefly one of service, either at the

9 Lagny, p. 61.

original Reuilly house or one of the adjoining buildings, or at the different "stations" which have gradually been established in the course of the development of the deaconesses' work.

Yet community prayer is not thereby neglected. Though details of the original specific daily program have not come down to us, it is certain that from the beginning there was daily a sort of "family worship," including hymns, prayers, and reading. Every Sunday the sisters now have a special afternoon service, inspired in form by early liturgical traditions.

From the beginning, greatest care has been taken of the training of the young sisters. Again and again in the course of the years the attention of the community authorities has been directed to establishing a proper balance between the purely religious training of the postulants and the technical training necessary for the various tasks which await them. At the end of the training period—varying a great deal in length—the sisters are consecrated in a formal ceremony in which they bind themselves to the religious life. At the community of deaconesses at Reuilly, this commitment is made for a definite time only—two years, for example—and is indefinitely renewable.

In July of 1844 the Reuilly community acquired a large building in the Rue de Reuilly for their various activities, taking occupancy in 1845. It is there that the mother house is located today.

As may be gathered from the foregoing information, not all the deaconess movements of the nineteenth century belong only to the past of the Protestant Church. In France, the Reuilly community continues its work at numerous stations, both in Metropolitan France as well as in mission territory. In Germany, the deaconesses number almost fifty thousand in their one hundred and twenty communities or associations. Of course not all these associations constitute religious communities properly speaking; yet others reveal very little difference between their essential plan of life and that of religious communities properly speaking with which we shall deal later in this volume. Thus, for example, the Bethlehem community at Hamburg follows a Rule[10] which seems quite significant in this connection.

On the basis of a specific calling to the work of the deaconesses,

10 Cf. *La Diaconesse*, review of the Reuilly deaconesses, April–June, 1957, pp. 12–18.

detailed directions on the sisters' three services, or tasks, are given in their rule:

Service in the Word of God and Prayer

We read and meditate personally on Sacred Scriptures every day, so as to be nourished, strengthened, and directed by the Word of God itself.

The deaconess pursues this reading and this meditation with fidelity, calling upon the Holy Spirit for help. For this she imposes upon herself her own personal rule, which proves an effective aid.

In the course of her days she observes periods of withdrawal and silence, set aside for the Word of God: especially in the morning, before the busy tasks of the day; and in the evening, when the work day is over. It is also useful to stop for a moment in the course of the day for a brief recollection.

Should the reading or meditation of the Word of God become a burden, or turn into a superficial routine, let the deaconess seek the advice and help of some tried and true Christian.

When a deaconess is called upon to bring the message of the Word of God to someone else, let her be the first to bow before the Word which she is about to read or comment on.

In every circumstance let the deaconess recall that, of the Scriptures, Christ himself said: It is they which give testimony of me.

God's commandment and his promises require of us the daily service of prayer. We bring to God thereby the homage due his Majesty, and place our lives under his judgment and his grace.

The life of the deaconess is led in the world, for the service of man, but it is at the same time the service of God. Now prayer is the principal service of God.

The deaconess realizes that in prayer she is united with the choirs of angels and saints of God. She is no less united with the whole Church, which lifts her prayer aloft from the earth, towards God.

Profiting by the long experience of the Church, she reserves for prayer certain fixed hours in the course of her day. When time, or strength, is deficient, she raises to God at least a word of praise, a supplication, or an Our Father.

She tries to enter body and soul into her prayer, brings to it all the outward signs, too, of a recollected and humble fervor before the majesty of God, and imbues it with all the generous impulse of a self-sacrificing soul.

If she finds hereself relaxing in the service of prayer, let her see in this a temptation and a trial. Let her appeal earnestly and conscientiously for the succor of the Church. Let her realize that she is surrounded by the prayer of the children of God, and supported above all by that of the high priest, Jesus Christ, who said to his disciple: I have prayed for thee, that thy faith fail not.

Service of the Kingdom of God by Celibacy,

Poverty, and Obedience

We know that God grants, and blesses, the renouncement—for the sake of his Kingdom—of marriage, motherhood, and family; and we witness with gratitude the Holy Spirit's diffusion, in the Church, of the gift of celibacy.

The deaconess sees a vocation from God in her unmarried state, and undertakes to follow it as a "servant of the Lord." She has the joyous certainty that Jesus has made her an associate of his own life, has determined to let her lack for nothing, and will lead her to the glorious peace of heavenly rest.

She realizes that she is called to a love of God which fills her whole life, and to a motherly gift of herself to those whom she seeks to serve, and to love with the Lord's own love.

In the temptations of the single life, she has fraternal support and spiritual comfort to fall back upon; she will experience that God's design is to give her a soul strong with peace and joy; and she will ask herself whether she has done everything needful to remain, in accordance with the apostle's counsel: in the state that was hers when the Lord called her.

We are convinced that the call to renounce every earthly possession is one that should be more widespread in the Church, and that the Lord Jesus Christ can render serviceable to himself the offering of everything a man has in his possession or at his disposal.

The deaconess is intent upon rendering her service without preoccupation either with merits to be gained or with personal advantages to be secured. Thanks to the non-remuneration of her work she is placed beyond the scramble for pay increases and professional advancement, and can devote herself to her task with no ulterior motives.

Whatever goods of this world belong, or are simply intrusted, to her she possesses as if she did not possess them. She seeks to combine decency and comeliness with simplicity and sobriety so that no one is ever self-conscious in her presence.

If gifts are offered her on the occasion of her service, she tactfully explains that since she receives everything gratuitously, she must give everything gratuitously, too. She may suggest that the gift be given, instead, to some Christian cause, or to her community. Personally, she enjoys practicing the art of expressing a bountiful heart by means of little marks of attention.

The deaconess is on the watch against becoming the slave of mediocre desires, wretched ambitions, and annoying habits. She receives her nourishment with gratitude, is happy with what she has, and seeks nothing more. When she fasts, she follows the injunctions of the Gospel, with none but interior motives.

By her renunciations, and by her offerings of self, the deaconess attests that God is the only real good which is worth being attached to. Her refuge is the Lord's promise: Blessed are the poor in spirit; the kingdom of heaven is theirs.

Our desire is to live in a state of evangelical obedience, that is, one based on the bonds which our Lord Jesus Christ established between God and his children, and among these children themselves. Thus we seek the will of God in the expressed will of those to whom he has bound us.

The deaconess is ever mindful that the Word of God describes faith as an obedience, and sin as a disobedience; she seeks to make of her obedience a visible sign of the obedience of faith.

Perfect Readiness in Service of Neighbor

In imitation of her Lord, the deaconess addresses herself with the same spirit to big and little tasks; and makes it a point of honor to stoop to the insignificant, the humble, the rejected, the scorned. . . .

The deaconess tries to render everyone his due, and always with kindness and patience. . . . She shows herself careful to see that everything is done as equitably as possible; yet she seeks, relying firmly on God, to silence every contentious or litigious spirit. . . . In every circumstance she calls to mind the words of St. Paul: Everything is yours, but you are Christ's.

Then the rule concludes in part:

This rule is meant as a testimony of our plan of life and service. We intend, individually or in community, to reread it often, in order to bring our lives and our service ever more fully in harmony with the cause, the tenor, and the purpose of our vocation.

May God in his goodness grant that we progress towards the fulness that is in him alone.

To the account just given of the deaconess community movement mention must be added of certain communities of men, like the Diakonenanstalt Nazareth at Bethel, near Bielefeld, the Brotherhood of the Common Life of Rüschlikon, in Switzerland, and the Diakonieverein attached to it.

We have in all this indisputably a profound religious movement, and a concrete response, drawn from the Gospel, to certain urgent problems confronting the Christian conscience, or to—more exactly—certain human needs to which Christians may not remain indifferent. This response took the form of associations of Christians which did, assuredly, revive a certain number of characteristics of the active religious life. It does seem to us, however, that—in general, and without taking into account the present-day tendencies in accordance with which the deaconess movement is developing—we do not find in them religious communities, properly so-called, living by a rule—communities such as the twentieth century has seen develop in the realm of Protestantism, as we shall discover in the chapter which follows here.

Chapter II

CENOBITIC REVIVAL

Taizé, First Community of Men

AMONG present-day Protestant religious communities, the most important and the best known is Taizé. Several times in the course of the last few years it has been covered by illustrated periodicals, and has been the subject of television broadcasts. Books and pamphlets issuing from Taizé give evidence of the theological work being conducted there; and a number of phonograph records have provided examples of the office as chanted at Taizé. Despite the resultant familiarity, we believe it will be of use to present here the essential characteristics of this community.

1) History

In 1939, while he was a theology student at Lausanne, Roger Schutz got some friends together in a joint project, sustained by prayer in common, to organize study clubs and spiritual retreats under the form of a sort of third order for laymen. This was given the name of Great Community. Some house was evidently needed to provide a place for these activities. Since the war had come along, Roger Schutz decided, in August of 1940, to part temporarily from his friends and to look for such a house in France, in order to provide a center of spiritual activity in the very midst of the human distress in that period.

Among several possibilities, he chose a large residence in Bourgogne which had been empty for several years, in the almost abandoned village of Taizé. Once installed, all by himself he undertook

83

for two years to shelter in this isolated house refugees who crossed the line of the occupied zone nearby, the while he mulled over his resolution to set up in this village, once peace had returned, a community of young men bent upon consecrating their lives "to a service in common of Jesus Christ in the Church and in the world." Since those beginnings, a regular life of prayer—the divine office—has underlain this active life.

Very soon the first ecumenical contacts here were begun: Father Couturier and Father Villain came to Taizé as early as the summer of 1941.

It was in 1942, in Geneva, that Roger Schutz met three students— Max Thurian, Pierre Souvairan, and then Daniel de Montmollin, and was joined by them. Together they lived two years as a community, in an apartment, where they were visited by numerous friends. A life of prayer continued to sustain this existence, intended as a presence in the world and amidst its problems; and the morning and evening office were recited either in their common residence or in a chapel of the Saint-Pierre cathedral.

When the liberation came, during the summer of 1944, the community was able to take up quarters in Taizé. Thereupon it opened a children's home, The Manor, organized spiritual retreats, maintained contact with earlier associates, and developed ecumenical relationships with Christians of every belief, and particularly with the Catholic clergy and laity of the neighborhood.

Several years passed before stable new vocations enabled the original brothers of the community to make their profession; this they did on Easter morning of 1949. Here was a new and important step in the life of the community, marking the absolute character of a vocation which was to bind men for their entire lives to the service of God and their fellow men, in celibacy, common ownership of property, and submission to authority. The brothers had realized in effect that residence in a community could not endure stably without this threefold commitment on the part of its members. Just as a family community—as understood from the Christian point of view— cannot exist without a mutual and lifelong commitment on the part of man and wife, neither can a religious community be substantial and permanent without a permanent bond among the brothers— such a bond as insures their being able to count upon one another.

From that time on, new vocations were due to swell the size of the community, and to provide it with a potential for new services outside Taizé. In 1951 and 1952, mission brothers were sent out for the first time to various locations where, by their work and their life, they were to be "witnesses of Christ, . . . a sign of his presence among all men, and bearers of joy." The first mission fraternity of this kind, composed of two or three brothers, was sent out to a working-class neighborhood to live under wage-earners' conditions, first at Montceau-les-Mines, then at Marseilles. Others were to go later into the shanty-towns of Algeria, to a student center in Germany, to Paris for collaboration with CIMADE (refugees' and prisoners' aid), and into various parishes in France and Switzerland for pastoral work.

All the brothers return periodically to Taizé for the principal Christian feasts and for an annual retreat week in common. The house at Taizé is not only the scene of the daily activities of the brothers who reside there permanently, but is also becoming more and more a center for studies and for training, especially of the new brothers, who have at least two years of novitiate before making final profession. Mission brothers can come there and make a retreat, as to a sort of spiritual fueling point.

The most striking thing about the constitution of this community is the fact that it was never a clearly defined a priori attempt to imitate some Catholic order or some Eastern monastery. Without knowing exactly where the experience would lead them, the brothers at first joined together simply to lead the life of the Gospel in common. From that point on, as they now recognize, they were feeling their way: Were they, as some of them hoped, to create within the Reformation Churches some form of contemplative life, thus rendering primarily the service of prayer? Or were they, rather, to carry into the workaday world—particularly where the Word of God found no echo—testimony of Christ's activity and his presence? What were to be the bonds of each brother with the community? Were they to be purely spiritual, and fundamentally revocable? Or were they, instead, to involve some sort of obligation of a solemn engagement? Thus, it was no a priori conception, but experience of the needs of our times and the meditation in common on the Gospel that led the brothers to give definite form to their original vocation and their way of life.

2) The rule

In 1952 and 1953 Roger Schutz edited the *Rule of Taizé*, a spiritual document redolent of the Gospel, inspired by the common life of the first years, and laying down the fundamental directives of a vocation which combines the monastic experience of Christians of both West and East, and plunges its roots through the Reformation into the life of the Church's first centuries. This same rule was also adopted in November, 1953, by the Grandchamp community.

It is more a program of life than a set of regulations in the narrower sense of this word; and for this reason the brothers have found in it the original inspiration of all monastic or religious rules. As the rule itself makes clear,

> There is a danger in having indicated in this Rule only the minimum necessary for the common life. It is better to run this risk and not to confine oneself in complacency and routine.

The rule is not to be understood as a "law" which would contravene evangelical liberty:

> If this Rule were ever to be regarded as an end in itself and to dispense us from ever more seeking to discover God's design, the love of Christ, and the light of the Holy Spirit, we would be imposing on ourselves a useless burden. Then it would have been better never to have written it.

After the preamble, the Rule has four sections:

a) Community activities: prayer, meals, assembly, and order in the community.

b) Spiritual discipline.

c) The commitments: celibacy, common ownership of property, and submission to authority: the prior.

d) Mission brothers; new brothers; guests.

The Rule concludes with the text of the exhortation which is read at the ceremony of profession.

The preamble insists above all on the integration of the brothers into the community ("From now on you are no longer alone. You must in all things take your Brothers into account"), and on their common progress towards Christ as a condition of their true spiritual liberty: "Never come to a halt; go forward with your Brothers; run toward the goal in the footprints of Christ."

From the very first pages, the two dominant notes of their vocation are heard:

a) Presence in the world: "Open yourself to that which is human and you will see all vain desire to flee from the world vanish from your heart. Be present to your day and age."

b) Ecumenicism: "Never resign yourself to the scandal of the separation of Christians, all of whom so easily profess love for their neighbor, yet remain divided. Be consumed with burning zeal for the unity of the Body of Christ."

Among the activities of the community, prayer occupies the first place; whether this be prayer in common or "personal" prayer, it is equally a community activity. Since prayer is a human act, it must be clothed with signs and expressed through them, though of course not so muffled with signs that the thing signified is smothered. Prayer must continue throughout all the chores of the day; it must be "the participation of our whole being in the work of God through our intelligence and our lips."

The community meal is considered one of the essential activities of the common life; here "our brotherly love is manifested." This notion is conceived in the light of the meals which the Lord ate with his disciples, and the fraternal repasts of the first Christians in Jerusalem.

Another occasion instinct with fraternal life is the assembly, in which all professed brothers take part.

> The purpose of the Council is to seek all the light possible concerning the will of Christ for the advance of the Community. . . . Nothing is more contrary to the spirit of the Council than search which is not purified by the sole desire to discern God's will.

At the assembly, the brothers are invited to give their opinions, but, "To avoid one seeking to outdo another in argument, the Prior is responsible before his Lord for making the decision without being bound by a majority."

Finally, regard for the common good must take the form of a certain minimum of order in the community:

> Therefore there is no excuse for disturbing one's Brothers by unpunctuality. Consider the lack of fervor your negligence reflects. . . . Never be an obstacle through lack of zeal in rejoining Brothers with whom you have engaged yourself totally, in body and spirit.

7

The activities of the community having been set forth, there remains to be specified the spirit in which they are to be performed. Hence the three spiritual disciplines:

> In your day let both work and rest be enlivened by the Word of God. In everything, guard interior silence, so as to remain in the presence of Christ. Immerse yourself in the spirit of the Beatitudes: joy, simplicity, mercy.

The brothers' life is basically directed by meditation on the Word of God and by prayer. "Let each hour have the prayer, work, or rest assigned to it; but all must be in God."

This submission to the Word of God entails each brother's keeping interior silence.

> Inward silence requires first to forget one's self, to quiet discordant voices, and to master obsessing worry, in the perpetual recommencement of one who is never discouraged because always forgiven.
>
> There are moments when the silence of God culminates in his creatures. In the solitude of the retreat, we are renewed by intimate meeting with Christ. These essential moments must therefore be reserved.

Probably the thing that strikes anyone who is visiting or making a retreat here are the three beautitudes in accordance with which the community is determined to live: joy, simplicity, and mercy.

> Perfect joy is in the laying aside of self in peaceful love. . . . For it is often at the bottom of the abyss that perfection of joy is given in communion with Jesus Christ. . . . It is wonderment continually renewed in face of the free giving of Him who grants an abundance of spiritual and material benefits. It is thankfulness. It is thanksgiving.
>
> Your availability implies continual simplification of your existence, not by constraint, but by faith. . . . Recognize your mistakes with simplicity, in the transparency of brotherly love, without finding therein a pretext for discerning those of the others. . . . [Simplicity] is found in the free joy of a Brother who forsakes obsession with his progress or backslidings, in order to fix his gaze on the light of Christ.

As for mercy, the brothers, far from finding obstacles in the chance difficulties and antipathies that may exist among them, try to let themselves be caught up—without any affected sweetness—"by a superabundance of friendliness towards all." Each must be a leaven of unity, but without simply closing his eyes to the shortcomings of others:

> If you fear you may flatter the pride of a Brother by overlooking his

offense, then exhort him, but always with him alone and with the gentleness of Christ. If you fail to do so, in order to preserve your desire for influence or for popularity with certain Brothers, you are a stumbling block within the Community.

If you have doubts as to the attitude of a Brother, and either you cannot express them to him or he refuses to listen, confide them to the Prior, who will consider with you how to act and to help this Brother. If he refuses to listen to you, report the matter to the Community.

It is also in light of this beatitude that the brothers practice personal confession.

Because of the weakness of your flesh [flesh understood here not in the sense of the material substance, but in the Pauline sense of "the old man"], Christ gives you visible and repeated signs of his forgiveness. Absolution restores you to the joy of salvation. . . . The sin of a member marks the whole body, but God's forgiveness re-establishes the sinner within the Community. Confession is made to one and the same Brother, chosen with the Prior.

It is no doubt not without significance that it is only after a careful definition of the spirit according to which the brothers are to live that any consideration is given in the Rule to the commitments to which they subscribe at the time of their profession. It is to be noticed, moreover, that the limits fixed by the spiritual disciplines rigorously exclude any understanding of these commitments as a human meriting of salvation, or as a way of life in any degree superior to the ordinary Christian one.

As for celibacy, as St. Paul emphasized, it "brings greater availability to concern oneself with the things of God." But the brothers are to see in it, not a superior state of life, but a formal gift of self to others: "It is to be taken only for the sake of a great gift of self— with Christlike love—to one's fellow men." Here it is actually this whole chapter of the Rule which should be cited, in the course of which is explained, in accordance with the quotation above, the real value of a celibacy which

means neither breaking with human affections, nor indifference, but calls for the transformation of our natural love. . . . When the selfishness of the passions is not surpassed by growing generosity; when you no longer use confession to defeat the need, contained in all passion, to assert yourself; when your heart is not constantly filled with an immense love; you can no longer let Christ love within you and your celibacy will become a burden.

This transformation of natural love is nothing but a purification of the heart, for which immense patience and constant effort are necessary. "To live in the continual recommencement of the Christian who is never overcome because always forgiven," to be frank with others, to reject every vulgarity, to guard against typical bachelor slovenliness—these are conditions necessary for a progressive purification.

Purity of heart can only be lived in spontaneous and joyous forgetfulness of self in order to lay down one's life for those whom one loves. This gift of oneself implies the acceptance of a sensibility often deeply wounded. There is no friendship without purifying suffering. There is no love of one's neighbor without the Cross. The Cross alone makes known the unsearchable depths of love.

As for common ownership of property, it is a total one, and extends even to trifles. It involves living

in the present moment . . . without assurance of the morrow, in joyous confidence that they will lack for nothing. The spirit of poverty does not consist in pursuing misery, but in setting everything in the simple beauty of creation. If God gives freely the good things of the earth, it is blessed for man to give that which he has received.

The rule speaks of submission to authority—the prior:

There is no hope of a bold and total service of Jesus Christ without unity of mind. . . . The prior focusses the unity of the Community. . . . The Brothers should remain spontaneous with him, . . . By their trust the Brothers renew the Prior in the seriousness of his vocation for the joy of all; . . . Let each Brother, privately, make his fears known to the Prior.

It is thus that the prior (with the help of the assembly in matters of greater importance) is enabled, not to subject souls to himself, but instead, "to build up the whole body in Christ," by respecting the particular vocation of each brother, and by helping him—firmly but mercifully—to correspond with that vocation in this particular community.

Brothers out on mission are to live in the same spirit as those at Taizé. "The witness of all is involved by their attitude. They keep the Prior regularly informed of their life." Generally they go out by twos, threes, or fours: rarely alone.

"In order to be trained in the school of Christ, the new Brother has need of sound biblical and human nurture." The concern of all the brothers is to "cause them to progress in the love of Jesus Christ." One brother has been selected to be responsible for their training.

> It is Christ himself whom we receive in a guest. . . . Let hospitality be liberal and exercised with discernment. . . . A Brother is appointed to take care of the guests.

The Rule ends with the exhortation read by the Prior at every profession:

> Brother, you who commit yourself to God's mercy, remember that the Lord Christ comes to strengthen your feeble faith and that, covenanting with you, he fulfills for you the promise: Truly, there is no one who has given up home, or brothers, or sisters, or mother, or father, or wife, or children, or land, for my sake and for the Gospel, who will not receive in this age a hundred times as much—houses, and brothers, and sisters, and mothers, and children, and land—and persecutions besides; and in the age to come eternal life.
>
> This is a way opposed to all human reason, but like Abraham, you can advance on this way only by faith, not by sight, always assured that he who loses his life for Christ's sake shall find it.
>
> Henceforth walk in the steps of Christ. Do not be anxious about tomorrow. Seek first God's kingdom and his justice. Surrender yourself, give yourself, and good measure, pressed down, shaken together, and running over, will be poured into your lap; for the measure you give is the measure you will receive.
>
> Whether you be waking or sleeping, by night and by day, the seed sprouts and grows, you know not how.
>
> When you pray, do not use vain repetitions like the heathen, who think they shall be heard for their many words.
>
> Do not display your righteousness before men to win their admiration. Do not let your inward discipline give you a sorrowful appearance, like a hypocrite who puts on an unsightly face so that he may be seen of men. Anoint your head, wash your face, so that only your Father who is in secret might know the intention of your heart.
>
> Maintain yourself in simplicity and in joy, the joy of the merciful, the joy of brotherly love.
>
> Be vigilant. If you are to admonish a Brother, let it be between yourself and him alone.
>
> Always seek fellowship with your neighbor.
>
> Confide; know that a guide must watch on behalf of your soul, as one who must render account. Be understanding toward him, so that he may fulfill his ministry with joy.
>
> The Lord Christ, in his pity and his love for you, has chosen you to be a sign of brotherly love within the Church. He wills that with your Brothers you should realize the parable of the Community.

Thus, renouncing henceforth all thought of looking back, and joyful
with infinite gratitude, never fear to precede the dawn
> to praise
> and bless
> and sing
> *Christ your Lord.*

3) Taizé today

The community of Taizé counted, at the beginning of the year
1960, two score brothers from various Reformation Churches in
both the Lutheran and Calvinist lines. They are of various national-
ities: French, Swiss, Dutch, German, and so forth. Half reside at
Taizé; the rest are in Marseilles, Algiers, Valentigney, Ivory Coast,
Germany, and the United States of America.

Both in Taizé and outside it, the brothers' activity is always dominated by a double aim: to be present both in the Church and in the
world.

They are present in the Church through the contemplative life and
the daily office, by the frequent celebration of the Eucharist, by an
ardent prayer that Christians be granted visible unity in the Body
of Christ, and by a ministry of meetings with, and overtures towards,
Christians of all denominations.

> Future generations will be less and less willing to accept the contradic-
> tion of Christians divided into different creeds. They will no longer
> tolerate the waste of the energies expended in justifying credal stand-
> points at a time when, because of the staggering growth of populations,
> the number of men who do not know God grows larger every day.
> They will no longer put up with a situation in which Christians spend
> their best efforts proving the solidity of the foundations which support
> their particular opinions.[1]

> Without prayer for unity the work of ecumenism will be dry and
> hollow. When we encounter the difficulties erected by sin and human
> traditions on both sides and when our progress is halted by the deep-
> seated differences which are constantly emerging, prayer can revive our
> hope and love. When we pray for unity we ask the mercy of the Lord.
> We humble ourselves for our faults and for the obstacles which we our-
> selves place in the way. We intercede for all of those who work especially
> for unity, that in and through God they may become instruments of
> unity.[2]

1 Roger Schutz, Prior of Taizé, *Living Today for God* (Helicon, 1962), p. 71.
2 Schutz, p. 81.

The brothers are present in the world by virtue of their way of life, and by virtue of their resolution to live by the work of their hands, to assume professional responsibilities, to dwell among the outcasts of fortune, and to bring the Gospel to life at the crossways of the world.

We must strive for a Christian engagement in the human society around us. We must discover in our own field, in our place of work, the means of radiating—perhaps without a word—the presence of Christ. For you must accept a man where you find him, how you find him, in order to enter into his humanity and understand him from within. In such an acceptance it will no longer be a question of judging him but only of loving him with a love that understands everything. The world, which knows little of the Gospel, knows that we profess a fraternal love among all men and on the strength of this often makes astonishing demands upon us. We must remain sensitive to these demands in order to respond to them. The younger generation has a thirst for the authentic. It hates trickery and Christian pharisaism and will not tolerate ready-made solutions. Our Christianity must be rooted in the concrete situations of today's world.[3]

It is in this perspective that the community has decided to place its mission brothers in Negro Africa, in the midst of the Moslem populations in Algiers, and in the working-class milieu in Marseilles: an insignificant handful of men employing their small resources to bring the presence of the Church to a few street-corners of the workaday world.

It is the same perspective that governs the activity of the brothers who stay at Taizé; their professional life exercises a similar presence in the world. Alongside ecumenical theology and retreat work, various other fields—farming and agricultural unions, work in printshop and art studio, rural medical practice and church architecture—are also points of contact with the world of today.

Besides being a place for prayer, study, and theological thought, Taizé is also a crossroads and meeting place serving continuing ecumenical interests (experience has shown the necessity of such association, the continuity of which a monastic community can suitably provide); frequent journeys serve to keep up and extend these ecumenical contacts, and permits the particularism of local problems to be surmounted by a view of wider horizons.

3 Schutz, pp. 66, 67.

It is in order to step up this necessary activity, and to bring itself closer to the center of the tension between Church and world, that the Taizé community has, for example, taken the initiative in the "Rencontres de Cormatin," sociological study sessions conducted a few miles from Taizé.

And the spiritual climate in which all this life is to be lived is admirably described in these lines:

> If we are to remain ardent in God's present day, the living charity of Christ must come and fan the flame within us and renew our friendship for our neighbor, our brother.[4]

> We can accomplish wonderful works, but only those will count which proceed from the merciful love of Christ within us. At the end of our lives we will be judged according to love, the love which we have allowed to grow little by little and to spread itself out in compassion for every man living in the Church and in the world.[5]

The Grandchamp Community

ALL that we have said of the spirituality of Taizé can be applied to the community at Grandchamp (near Neuchâtel in Switzerland), where a similar vocation for women has taken concrete form.

The Grandchamp community is the result of retreat work conducted there, an activity which has lately become one of the essential characteristics of its service to the Church.

In 1931, for the first time, a few women—seeking to deepen their spiritual life so as to give witness in their daily life and in the Church —gathered in a house in the hamlet of Grandchamp for three days of prayer, silence, and meditation. One of them, Mme. Léopold Micheli, was to become, thirteen years later, Sister Genevieve, the Mother of the community.

But already in 1936 a retreat house was opened at Grandchamp by Sister Margaret, who, aided by Sister Martha, thereafter received guests the year around who wanted a place in which to adore and pray in silence. As the years passed, the retreats multiplied. In 1940, Sister Irene joined the other two, and together, besides devoting their time to this ministry of prayer, they undertook a life of personal poverty.

---

4 Schutz, p. 123.
5 Schutz, p. 128.

In 1944, the three called upon Sister Genevieve for aid. Then several new vocations enriched the budding community. On the tenth anniversary of the opening of the retreat house, Pastor Marc du Pasquier, presiding minister of the Church of Neuchâtel, defined their ministry when he spoke of the "Upper Room of the Church." In the following years, 1947 and 1948, the growth of retreats and the requirements of the liturgical life demanded more housing space, and the group acquired several of the houses in the hamlet. Moreover, the Spiritual Retreat Foundation was set up, and attached to the Protestant Federation of Churches of Switzerland.

From 1950 to 1954 the ministry of Pastor Jean de Saussure as chaplain of the community produced the notable result of the development of the liturgical life as a basis of all the current and future activity there. Midway in this period, the profession of the first eight sisters and the formal installation of Sister Genevieve as Mother of the community in 1952 marked the completion of this twenty-year-long road to the establishment of a cenobitical community of women with lives consecrated to the exclusive service of God.

The identity of vocations here and at Taizé is obvious. The points of departure and the roads were different: but they led to the recognition of the same basic ministry in the Church and in the world. For this reason, the Grandchamp community, in 1953, adopted the rule of Taizé; and in November of that year there was a meeting of the two communities at Grandchamp. The prior of Taizé and Sister Genevieve drafted a document according to which the two communities declared "their common vocation to the service of Jesus Christ, and the unity of their witness within the Churches of the Reform." Thenceforth the prior of Taizé was to provide or suggest new initiatives for the development of Grandchamp (in matters of ministries of fraternity, for example); the periods of retreat and reflection for sisters (or annual probation) were to be directed by a brother; unity in thought, prayer, and activity were to be further manifested and strengthened.

Today there are about thirty sisters, assigned to three groups: those who stay at Grandchamp; those who make up the resident community of the Sonnenhof hospice at Gelterkinden; and the mission sisters, in small establishments of two or three in places where human misery bespeaks a special need of the presence of Jesus Christ.

The principal work of the resident communities of Grandchamp
and Gelterkinden is to receive guests and to organize retreats.
Whereas at Taizé retreats are individual, at Grandchamp and Gelterkinden group retreats are customary. At the Grandchamp and Sonnenhof houses, the retreats—sometimes open to all, sometimes restricted to certain categories of Christians (missionaries, pastors'
wives, married couples, and so forth)—last for four or five days and
are under the direction either of a pastor or of one of the brothers
of Taizé. The retreatants are given a certain number of biblical or
spiritual talks, which provide a framework for their periods of reflection and prayer.

In connection with Taizé and Grandchamp a Third Order of Unity
has been established. This is a group of men and women who wish
to profit by the spirituality of the rule of Taizé, without the obligations entailed in actual residence in the community. In the Third
Order the same two aims as in the communities themselves are
dominant: presence in the Church through prayer for unity and
through a ministry of ecumenical contacts, and presence in the world
by prayerful participation in one's social milieu.

The Retreat of Pomeyrol

To a discussion of Taizé and Grandchamp must be added an account
of the Retreat of Pomeyrol.

The Pomeyrol community, where the spirit of poverty is the most
important characteristic, is of comparatively early origin. The superior, Mlle. Antoinette Butte, began this ministry in a retreat house
opened in November of 1929 at Saint-Germain-en-Laye. There, in
connection with a modest oratory, amid very great material difficulties, retreats were organized for people seeking silence, prayer, and
solitude. The plan of these retreats largely followed, in spirit and
practice, the devotions of the Third Order of Watchers.

At the beginning of the war, Mlle. Butte had to give up the house
at Saint-Germain-en-Laye when it was requisitioned for national
defense needs. Thereupon she found quarters at Pomeyrol; and
during the following winter the first attempt at community life
properly speaking got under way there.

With the Liberation, the property at Pomeyrol was not spared.

It was occupied in turn by the F.F.I. and by an Arab refugee center. Only in March, 1946, was it turned back to the Retreat. The first task then was to set to rights the grounds and the house, which had undergone an astonishing amount of damage at the hands of the various occupants. The chateau was then converted into a home for abandoned children and placed in charge of friends of the Retreat. The sisters themselves occupied the barracks that had been put up in the yard by the Germans; and it is here that they are at this present day, while retreatants are generally received in what was the hunting lodge.

The primary obligation of this (numerically negligible) community is prayer. The services are inspired both by older liturgical traditions —Orthodox, Anglican, or Roman Catholic—and by more recent forms of piety, especially those in use among the various Reform faiths. The sisters have appropriated from the liturgy of the Reformed Church of France as well as from the books of the Moravian Brethren and from the practices of the Quakers. They have published a sort of manual of "daily liturgy" in use at Pomeyrol for retreatants, in the preface of which we read:

> This liturgy uses the collection of hymns of the [Reformed] Church, and presupposes its Sunday liturgy. It has borrowed freely from liturgical elements belonging to various spiritual families of French Protestantism: to the Third Order of Watchers, it owes certain meditations, and the recitation of the Beatitudes at noon; to the Moravian Brethren, the practice of two short scriptural texts and special prayers for each day of the week; to the Federation of Students, certain prayers and their manner of intercesssion; to the Quakers and to Moral Rearmament, silent recollections followed by sharing; to the liturgies of Pastor Décopuet, the arrangement of services for major feasts. And, finally, there are adopted here the invocations and antiphonal prayers which the "Church and Liturgy" movement borrowed from the Roman, Eastern, and Anglican Churches; also the hymns of the Church of the first centuries are taken from the Roman breviary as a kind of continuation of the Psalter.

This novel liturgy is intended as a translation into forms of worship of a rediscovery of faith:

> Spontaneity, organic growth, creative burst of collective faith and prayer . . . such variety, such primitive youthfulness are the needs, we feel, of the contemporary world which is coming to birth, and of a Church which is renewing its youth.

At Pomeyrol, the sisters gather four times a day for common prayer. In the morning, when they get up, the office—after individual or community meditation on the Word of God—consists of an act of adoration, a Psalm, the *capitulum*, then after a space of silence an informal petition for the intention of each of the participants, the Our Father, another Psalm, a hymn, and finally, as a conclusion, an act of spiritual communion. At noon the office is quite brief, containing essentially the recitation or chanting of the Beatitudes, followed by the Creed and the Magnificat or Gloria. At nightfall, the sisters reassemble for the singing of a Psalm and a responsory, and to hear scriptural passages "read and prayed." The evening office concludes with a period of formal petition and of contemplation. At night, when the sisters retire, the office includes a hymn, meditation on the Word of God, a prayer of thanksgiving, examination of conscience, the Our Father, and a hymn of benediction. It is not impossible, by the way, that bit by bit the liturgy at Pomeyrol will tend to become identical with the liturgy at Taizé and Grandchamp.

The life of the sisters takes its inspiration from Grandchamp. Furthermore, the rule of Taizé has been adopted at Pomeyrol. As at Grandchamp, the sisters of Pomeyrol (after a period of probation) assume the definitive threefold commitment of common ownership of property, celibacy, and obedience.

The "Marienschwestern" of Darmstadt

THE *Ökumenische Marienschwesterschaft* (ecumenical sisterhood of Mary)[6] is of comparatively quite early origin, but it is worth the trouble to trace its history for the light thus cast on its particular significance.

In 1939, at the time when the position of Christians in Nazi Germany was becoming increasingly difficult, six young women happened to fall in with Klara Schlink, a young woman who at that time was giving courses in biblical training. These young people begged her to form a private biblical circle for the six of them. But a few months after this step the circle so organized had swelled to over a hundred participants. Not many years later, some of them were to be

6 The Darmstadt Sisters published in 1955 (with a revised edition in 1959) a brochure describing their community: *Ökumenische Marienschwesternschaft, Weg und Auftrag.*

members of the community of sisters which was the outcome—
though at the beginning no one, not even the guiding spirit of the
circle, had any idea of such a result. Somewhat staggered by the
growing number of participants, Klara Schlink appealed for aid to
her friend Erika Madauss, who (like herself) had turned down a
brilliant career in order to devote herself to the biblical ministry.

The circle led a momentous existence, being ever a prey to the
suspicions of the public authorities; the Nazi officials, however, were
powerless to put a halt to the circle's activities.

Then, on the night of September 11–12, 1944, a saturation bom-
bardment wiped out the city of Darmstadt. The members of the
biblical circle—they were already calling themselves sisters—saw in
this catastrophe the judgment of God upon their city, but especially
upon themselves. They became terribly aware, and more intensely
as week followed week, that no one is pure in the sight of God; and
they realized then, as an immediate and personal fact, the need for
repentance, for reparation, and for unceasing prayer. This vivid consciousness of the necessity of penance if they were to make up in
themselves "what is lacking in the passion of Christ for his Body"
became the leitmotiv of the little circle and was to produce a marked
effect on the future foundation. In their own recollection of those
moments:

> A new life surged through us, and waxed more intense day after day.
> We felt obligated, forced, to offer our prayers and petitions for our
> country; we were grasping the fact that repentance is not a single act,
> accomplished once and for all, but must be constantly renewed; when-
> ever we met we had such awful awareness of divine judgment that we
> were impelled to humble ourselves and confess our sins.

A few months after all this happened, at the very moment when
American troops were nearing Darmstadt, and when highway and
rail travel were virtually hopeless, about fifteen of the young women
belonging to the circle accompanied Erika Madauss into the neighboring countryside of Odenwald for a closed retreat. From these days
of prayers and penance came the germ of the idea that they should
remain together to accomplish this indispensable mission of prayer.
It began to strike them as more and more necessary to experience
daily their purification in the Blood of Christ through reciprocal
candor and the confession of their sins to one another (this impulse

was later to lead to the formal institution of a "chapter of faults").

During the hard months which followed, amid the many restrictions imposed on individual liberty in the first period of foreign occupation, they formed the habit of meeting one day a week, Wednesdays generally, for meditation on the Scriptures and for prayer. The atmosphere of these meetings—well, as the sisters tell us, it was that of the first community at Jerusalem, including the sharing of their few provisions, all surrendered to the common stock.

These weekly meetings made their desire to remain together a more definite one. In fact, numerous criticisms (sometimes a trifle bitter) leveled against these unusual meetings impelled them in the same direction, for this trial—as the sisters report—was the final confirmation needed for going ahead with their plan to form a permanent community. Under the guidance of the Reverend Paul Riedinger, of the Methodist Church, the sisters began to reside together as a community in 1947; there were at that time seven sisters, associated with the two mothers: Mutter Basilea (Klara Schlink) and Mutter Martyria (Erika Madauss).

The community began its existence under conditions of extreme poverty, in the narrow attic of Mutter Basilea's family home, with no furniture, no resources—and all this in the strictest rationing period. Without doubt there could have been no better school of the concrete gift of self than these difficulties. Poverty combined with close quarters to teach each individual sister the down-to-earth requirements of fraternal charity.

From the very start, each sister received her special charge in the community, while as a group they began their mission of popular preaching in all the most crowded places, especially the railroad station, and in the poorest neighborhoods of the city, not to speak of the women's prisons and reformatories.

It was at this time that they became aware of the part the community was to play in German Protestantism. It was to be a sign of God's love by daily living in complete dependence on the generosity of the heavenly Father and by sharing in the sufferings of Christ for his rent Body. In their missionary activity, it was to present evidence of the fact that it is only where there exists a community bound together by genuine love that the motivation and the stamina necessary for accomplishing this task can be found.

The community grew by leaps and bounds. In 1947 there were seven sisters; in 1952, fifty-eight, and two years later, sixty-six; and if, after 1954, this number did not increase, it was only because for the time being the community was being closed to new candidates.

As the figures just given suggest, by 1949 there was a painfully pressing need for larger and more independent quarters than Mutter Basilea's family home afforded. Since there was just no money for it, there could be no serious thought of building or even of acquiring already existent buildings. Such was the state of things when the father of one of the sisters came forward unprompted and offered a big-sized lot on the Heidelberg road in the suburbs of the city. This first sign from heaven, got by prayer, was followed by like ones— each time as a kind of surprise answer to the sister's prayers. Thus it was, for instance, that an architect came by one day to volunteer his services if ever the sisters should need them; and it was thus, too, that the sisters were granted permission to help themselves to the stones from bombed-out buildings to use for construction work.

Now, since the community had nothing to pay workmen with, it was decided that the sisters themselves should pitch in to a do-it-yourself operation under the foremanship of the kindly architect. Hard enough as it is, the work was all the harder under the postwar conditions then prevailing. Nevertheless, in a year and a half, there stood the chapel and the main residence buildings all finished. On Good Friday of 1951 the chapel was formally opened, and on September 7, 1952, quarters were in shape for the occupancy of the fifty-two sisters who then made up the community.

In 1954 the community was once more bursting at the seams, so up went the scaffolding again. Several times since then the growth of retreats and of new activities has sent the sisters back to their trowels and their saws, with which community members have now become seasoned hands.

To grasp what, exactly, the life of this community is, and in what its particular vocation consists, one almost has to see for one's self. Still, as we did in the case of Taizé, we can at least try to trace out here the distinctive lines of this community of the sisters of Darmstadt.

It is first of all a praying community. Several times a day the sisters gather in the chapel. In the morning, it is for a moment of informal prayer (this is a quite common practice in Reform churches). At noon, it is for prayers for the intention of Christian unity, and for Israel. In the first part of the afternoon, it is for meditation on the sufferings and death of Christ. And then, at night, it is for Vespers and Compline according to the rite of the Western Church.

Moreover, on Sunday morning they recite Lauds; and they take part in the Lord's Supper, which local and neighboring pastors take turns presiding at in the sisters' chapel. In fact, this common prayer is made continuous by the constant prayer of the community, and specifically, at each moment of the day, by the prayers of a pair of sisters in an interior chapel at their house. The members of the community relieve one another at hourly intervals, insuring this form of watch before the Lord (which recalls a practice of the Herrnhut brotherhood).

Not content with prayer in common, however, the sisters, each of them, must devote at least an hour a day to what they call conversation of love. This is, in more familiar terminology, mental prayer. Moreover, each sister has her especial intention, directing her penance and petitions: one, the Evangelical Church in Germany; another, the Orthodox Church; a third, the Roman Church; still another, the Pope; and so it goes—no faith but has its intercessor in this community, whose lifelong charge it has become. The mother superior herself spends the greatest part of her time in vocal and mental prayer, one cell and a private oratory being reserved to her for this assignment of intercession, which she considers a bedrock necessity.

As a praying community, it is by the same token a penitential one. From the very first, the community met to do penance in the name of the whole German people for all the evils for which the Germans were collectively responsible during the war years. Especially do they wish to take upon themselves the sufferings which any Germans may have caused the Jews during the Nazi regime.

Both in its prayers and in its penances, the community feels itself called to testify for Christian unity: it is intended as a hearthside where Christians of various faiths may meet, or as a truly living cell in the body of Christians progressing together towards unity. It was most of all for this purpose that they built their guest house. Here every little room has the name of one of the Christian faiths, and is especially devoted to it by means of the selection of photographs and pictures for the walls, the framed mottoes, and the books left there for the use of retreatants—all of which are an attempt to represent this particular faith authentically. And no doubt more than one Lutheran or Calvinist is surprised to find in the Roman Catholic room some text, for example, of John of the Cross, expressing the absolute transcendence and inaccessibility of God, just as the Catholic may marvel at a declaration on the part of Luther or some other Reformer concerning the Virgin Mary or the Church.

This same orientation is expressed through the numerous community publications which come off the sisters' printing presses, since most of these are devoted to the movement for Christian unity.

Finally, the community is also intended to be a missionary one. It is not content with exercising a spiritual ministry by means of retreats, though this work seems to it the essential one. The sisters are also willing to go outside their convent for the special task of bringing the Gospel to the unprivileged and the poor. For this purpose they acquired an old bus, which they transformed into a kind of mobile catechism classroom. Three or four of them make trips to the poorer sections or outskirts of the big cities to speak to children who for one reason or another do not have an opportunity to attend catechism classes or Sunday school. By so doing, they also reach the families of these children, attracted by this somewhat unusual—and extremely lively—method of preaching.

Nor do the sisters hesitate to drive their bus up to where there is a carnival, street fair, or other popular festivity, and making their pitch next to the shooting gallery, or the merry-go-round, or the roller-coaster, they recite—in a very lively and attention-getting way—their "stories," which are translations, into the language people actually talk, of the great parables of the Gospel.

For some years now, too, they have been making up a variety of stage shows, reminiscent of the medieval mystery plays, which they put on at home, in their chapel, but also in auditoriums in the large cities, with the idea of making the Gospel understandable by this means to people of today. Of course the aim of the sisters in this missionary work is not to win Christians over to the sisters' own particular faith, but rather to reawaken—or just to awaken—faith, and thus to direct each hearer toward his own particular belief.

8

Apart from these pictorial bits, if we are to try to characterize the spirituality of the Darmstadt sisters, we must note at once—as in the case of the Taizé brothers—their spirit of community: what they are doing is living together according to the Gospel, owning every thing in common—on the spiritual as well as on the material level.

As for spiritual community proprietorship, we note that everything is under the control of the mother foundress, Mutter Basilea. She is the concrete principle of unity in the community, perhaps sometimes in a way that comes close to being a trifle matriarchal.

As for material community proprietorship, the sisters live the spirit of poverty right up to the hilt. Rejecting every human device for balancing the budget, they live in daily dependence on the heavenly Father. It is to him, in a very practical manner, that they look each day for their daily bread, and it is with this idea that the sisters never accept any gainful employment: they receive everything free from the hand of the heavenly Father, so they likewise give everything free.

This spirit of poverty is pushed so far, in fact, that even for her personal needs a sister does not have to go to the community bursar for her necessities, but to God alone, who takes care of the matter in good season. The sisters feel themselves called to show, by this form of poverty, to a world entirely dominated by money and stocks and trust deeds and what have you, that God is a Father who makes even the smallest details of the needs of his children his business.

Finally, the sisters are unmarried. And here again they have a very definite notion of their chastity as calling upon them to give up any particular relationship in order to be free to serve both one another and their guests.

In the community, God himself is, so to speak, an almost tangible and quite familiar figure. In a way that is not far from being a little naive—a way, to be sure, reminiscent of the *Fioretti* of St. Francis of Assisi, for whom, by the way, the sisters have great veneration—God is mixed up in everything that happens in the house. Thus it is surprising to none of the sisters when from time to time, as the need requires, this figure intervenes in a miraculous fashion—for example, to restore to health almost instantaneously a sister who fell off a plank when the place was first abuilding, and was taken off, though without any hope, to the hospital.

Finally, a visitor cannot help being struck by the radiant joy of these sisters, and by their spiritual freshness. They may be conscious of having to bear, as penitents, the faults of their compatriots. But they also know—and they live in this knowledge—that, as the fault was amplified, grace has been more amply bestowed than ever.

Now we have presented, in the second part of this volume, a limited number of Protestant religious communities both in France and French-speaking territory and in Germany. Many other successes at cenobitical life might well have been described here, too.

Nor have we spoken of a certain number of institutions, variously founded, which, without being exactly regular communities, still represent certain experiments, certain steps, certain discoveries, all made in the genuine cenobitical spirit: we have in mind especially centers like Iona in Scotland, Agapè in Italy, the Ashram Protestants of India, Villemétrie near Paris, and the various communities in Germany attached to the Brothers of the Common Life.[7]

There are two main reasons why we have limited ourselves simply to listing a few examples of these.

On the one hand, it would be tiresome to read page after page of one monograph after another on communities which no doubt have individual interesting aspects but are in the main very much like one another.

On the other hand—and this is especially true of those that show the greatest differences—most of these centers are still wholly in the formative period. It would, doubtless, be interesting to catch as it were the living evolution which is causing them to turn from a group of friends, or from a group within a youth movement, into a fully established community. But that is the very danger—to mistake the transitional for the developed, to take for important certain developmental traits which, when the institution in question has attained its stability, will be revealed as only secondary. Finally, much would be out of date almost as soon as we could describe it.

Therefore, it is best not to speak of these groups in detail; it is fairer to them simply to mention their existence, and our interest in them, and to wait until a future date to treat of them at length.

---

7 On these various communities and experimental communities see René Beaupère, "Note conjointe," *Istina*, III (1956), pp. 304–312.

Part Three

THEOLOGICAL JUSTIFICATIONS

IN the first part of this work, we undertook a rapid survey of the thought of the Reformers on the subject of monastic and religious life. This survey enabled us to show the deep-rootedness of the rejection of monasticism and the vows on the part of most of the pioneers of the sixteenth-century Reformation.

In the second part of our book, we then presented certain facts which seemed at variance with those generally quite firm theoretical attitudes. Even in the Reformation Churches in the sixteenth and seventeenth century there were convents existing, and various experiments in this line were tried in the seventeenth century. In the nineteenth, various organizations for religious service set themselves up as communities. Finally, under quite new forms, religious communities based on the threefold commitment of celibacy, obedience, and common ownership of goods have made their appearance.

In this third part, therefore, we must now show how the facts we have examined find justification in Protestant thinking.

Is it by a rejection pure and simple of what the Reformers thought about the matter? For Protestants, we know, the thought of the Reformers (whatever its importance) is not in fact something binding; it is possible a priori—and the facts confirm this—to revise the declarations they made concerning this or that matter. Is this the case when it comes to vows and religious community life? And must we conclude from this that on this point the Churches born of the Reformation are returning little by little to a doctrine closer to Rome's than to Luther's or Calvin's? Or, instead, are present-day justifications for this religious revival still strictly within the margins of the "possibilities" left open—as something exceptional and extremely rare—by the Reformers themselves?

On the basis of the testimony offered by those who are themselves members of these communities, as well as on the basis of the attitudes of several Protestant theologians of the present day, we shall now attempt to answer this question.

Chapter I

THE COMMUNITIES AND
THE REAWAKENED CHURCH[1]

THE very first thing to be remarked is of an importance utterly fundamental if we are to understand, from the inside, the monastic revival
which we examined several examples of in the second part of this
volume. And that point is this: we have not been dealing here with
so isolated a phenomenon that it does not have any connection with

---

1 The use of the word "Church" in the chapters which follow calls for a few
distinctions. Since we are using it to set forth the thought of Protestant theologians, we must use it in the senses in which they use it themselves; we are not
in any way implying an ascription of a properly Catholic theological content to
the term.

The word as used here can designate three concrete entities:

(a) The parish: the local assembly gathered to pray and to hear the sermon; or
the extension of this sense to the group of Christians in a given locality who
regularly do or may so gather. The use of "Church" for "parish" is relatively
rare in Protestantism.

(b) The sociological entity, the administrative group, so to speak, made up of a
certain number of Christians who agree on a certain profession of faith, submitting to a common ecclesiastical jurisdiction, and having their own particular
organization, e.g., the Evangelical Church of Bavaria, the Reformed Church of
France. In this sense, quite common in Protestantism, we can use the word in
the plural (e.g., the World Council of *Churches*).

(c) All Christians taken together, without distinction of organization, or even
of profession of faith. Nevertheless, in the most current Protestant vocabulary,
this use of the word "Church" excludes, at least implicitly, the Eastern Orthodox
Churches and the Roman Catholic Church. It is in this sense that the rebirth
(or revival, or renewal) "of the Church" is spoken of.

(d) Finally, the word "Church" serves also to designate a mysterious entity,
which cannot be grasped by purely human experience, and which is made up of
the body of the elect.

contemporary Protestant history. We must emphasize with great insistence the fact that *the rediscovery of the religious life in Churches born of the Reformation is but one aspect of a general reawakening that has been going on in all the Churches since the beginning of the century.*

This general revival extends, in fact, to every sector of Christian life. It includes a theological and biblical revival, a liturgical revival, a missionary revival, and a revival above all of a study of the Church as such, accompanied by the birth and development of the ecumenical movement. The first thing we have to do, then, is to get this fact clear in our minds: the members of these Protestant religious communities are fully aware that they are participants in this general revival, and that their community life is precisely one of the forms it is taking.

Of course, chronologically—in the practical order—it is highly possible that in the concrete life of Reformation Churches these monastic revivals came first, and that they exercised an influence on the theological rediscoveries of our time.

In the theoretical order, however, it is the theological reawakening, manifold in expression, which underlies these modern-day concrete rediscoveries. We are therefore devoting a chapter here to a depiction of the manifold Christian reawakening, the context in which contemporary Protestant religious communities must be understood.

First, then, we may recall the basic crisis in nineteenth-century Protestant theology. As a result of the triumph of positive science, biblical studies became more and more critical, with the end result of a widespread humanization of the content of Christian doctrine. In general, though of course by no means exclusively, Christianity itself was tending to become a kind of higher humanism. Christ began to seem the Savior of mankind more as a result of having taught men how to live than as a result of the mystery of his death and resurrection. The Gospel as a rule of life began to consist more in an ethical attitude towards other people—a very fine attitude, of course, as a type of humanitarianism—than in an adherence to a transcendent, superrational doctrine. In other words, the Reformers' insistence on justification as coming from Someone Other than man himself ended up, after several generations, and under various influences that cannot be discussed here, in becoming a "justification" by man himself—a salvation of humankind through man's own effort, and finally, a religion of human nature.

Against this "liberalism"—often not devoid of sincere piety, by the way—there was at the beginning of this century a reaction on the part of a certain number of theologians, Karl Barth chief among them. Barth, it may be recalled, had been educated in the best of this liberal tradition. As a result, when faced with the duties of his pastoral office he found himself up against the question of what message he was to announce to his parishioners.

This question led him to restore to the foreground the real purport of the Bible: an existential message, utterly different from any ethical system, and proclaiming man's salvation in Christ Jesus, and the absolute sovereignty of God.

Thus it was as a result of his pastoral experience that Barth was led to reinstitute a vigorously dogmatic theology, and to make a capital point of God's intervention in—God's irruption into—human nature. Barth's work—which is still going on, since there are several volumes of his *Kirchliche Dogmatik* still to appear—attacked liberalism at the root. It disclosed a new direction for Protestant theology and biblical study to take: instead of viewing the Bible as a human book which expresses a "religious" attitude towards God, Protestant theologians and exegetes have undertaken to read it anew as a Luther or Calvin would read it, namely, as God's own word, directed to men, and announcing to them a mystery that transcends them, yet by which they are saved.

A whole series of exegetical and theological studies have brought back on the stage the great traditional articles of faith. In fact, a new reading of the Bible has moreover enabled many Protestants to free themselves from a certain number of dogmatic positions which the Reformers interpreted from the Sacred Scriptures and which successive generations of Protestants had continued to treat as capital. Compare, for example, Cullmann's exegetical and theological study of the text in St. Matthew (16:18), "Thou art Peter, and upon this rock I shall build my Church," with what Protestant authors of the preceding centuries had to say about this verse, and you will get a glimpse of the kind of thing we are referring to.

For another example, take the conception of the Lord's Supper which is gaining ground in Protestantism today, as witness the theses recently published by the *Evangelische Kirche in Deutschland*,[2] or more clearly still the recent *Foi et Constitution* studies on this subject. This conception has gone so far as to be totally contrary to the classical eighteenth-century Protestant understanding of the matter, and reconsiders aspects of it which were left wholly out of account by the Reformation.

The most striking example is the change in attitude towards the unity of the Church: the New Testament texts on the Church and on its unity are being understood in a wholly new way—to the extent in fact that the concrete attitude of the Protestant faiths in this regard has undergone a fundamental change.

This faith-inspired reading of the Bible as the word of God has led Protestantism to a keener realization of its proper "vocation," if one may speak thus, in fidelity to which it cannot cast itself in the role of possessor of the truth: for Protestantism remains open on principle—but in our day it has regained a full awareness of this principle—to a progressive reformation along the lines revealed by God's word. In a situation which he finds uncomfortable, the Protestant theologian feels himself constantly confronted by the word of God exactly as he discovers it in the Bible. Basically, it is as the effect of this faith-inspired confrontation with the word of God that we must understand the complex of tendencies and accomplishments which goes by the name of the reawakening of the Church.

On the level of the parishes themselves, this reawakening has taken the form first of all of a liturgical revival. This revival, we hasten to add, is not a more or less successful restoration of ancient ceremonies and rituals such as to turn divine worship into some sort of antique-shop show-window, which would interest a few *aficionados* but would fail to arrest the great mass of the faithful. Instead, it is a movement to give the Church—the assembled Christian community—a means of expression which corresponds, on the one hand, to the faith, and on the other, to the modern-day temper.

We may gather from the attempt to find means of expression for the Christian community that there has been a rediscovery of the fact that such a community does exist in the first place, and the significance of such a community for Christianity. Abandoning the

2 Cf. the commentary of R. Wolf accompanying the publication of these theses, in French, in *Positions luthériennes*, I (January, 1959).

ways of a deadly individualism, Protestant parishes have turned towards a more and more strictly and truly community life. No doubt that movement corresponds to an urge felt world-wide in every department of life today. But it is also the result of a return to the Gospel and to the Pauline conceptions according to which Christian life is inconceivable in the isolation of individualism. Understood as a community, the parish requires the collaboration of everybody: it is not just the pastor's business. It is literally true to say that it is everybody's business.

The Reformers established this fact in principle, based on the universal priesthood of Christians and the denial of a priesthood reserved to some individuals: theoretically, the least of the faithful in a Lutheran or Calvinist parish is as much a priest as the pastor. As a matter of fact, the life of Protestant parishes became highly "clericalized." Nowadays, however, there is a fairly general tendency towards a more tangible application of the Protestant doctrine of the priesthood.

Liturgical revival: the clearest proofs of it, certainly, are the publication, in various Protestant faiths, of new rituals. Thus the *Vereinigte Evangelisch-Lutherische Kirche Deutschlands* in 1956 published a new ritual containing not only the *Deutsche Messe* but also the offices of Vespers and Compline. Similarly, the *Eglise Réformée de France* has been perfecting a new official liturgy for the various church services.

The liturgical revival and the sacramental revival are of course inseparable. The Reformation, it is true, recognized but two sacraments. Without challenging the primary and basic place of these two —baptism and the Lord's Supper—Protestantism is going into the question of other "actions" and of their significance: confirmation, imposition of hands on the sick, and so forth. But it is above all on the subject of the two officially recognized sacraments that a full-scale program of research has been entered upon, and, within the parishes, an attempt begun to institute more authentic forms of celebration. Thus baptism, which was tending to become a strictly family ceremony, is regaining its place as an act of the Church, and there is an attempt to reintegrate it into public services and to emphasize its congregational significance.

As for the Lord's Supper, it is now celebrated more often. In

France, for instance, in parishes where twenty years ago it was celebrated no oftener than four times a year, it is generally celebrated at
least once a month, and in some places oftener. A similar change has
taken place in Germany.

Thus on the parish level the reawakening of the Church has taken
the form of spotlighting the meaning and importance of the community in Church worship, sacraments, and activity. It is also in the
parishes in the first instance that there is a conspicuous new awareness of the missionary vocation of a Christian. The dawn of com-
munity-consciousness in parishes has coincided with consciousness
of the Church as being "on mission." This awareness is still probably
keener in France than elsewhere: Catholic missionary movements
are trying to grapple with the problems presented by the very poor
spiritual condition of many Frenchmen; and Protestantism has been
similarly put to it to tackle, in accordance with its own principles,
this same problem.

But it is still probably more on the Church level that this renaissance of missionary consciousness is noticeable. By a strange over-
sight, Luther, Calvin, and more clearly still Melanchthon deleted
almost completely from among the duties of the Church the an-
nouncement of the mystery of salvation to far-off peoples. If their
position on this point is perhaps explicable in terms of certain tendencies—apparent or real—associated with more or less well understood Catholic missions over centuries of Christianity, it still does
not seem really evangelical to anybody today.

At any rate, the Churches produced by the Reformation have on
this point resolutely turned their backs upon the sixteenth-century
Reformers. As a matter of fact, Protestant missionary efforts were
fairly numerous from the time of Pietism on. We have seen on earlier
pages of this volume how Zinzendorf, founder of the Moravian communities of Herrnhut, was himself a missionary—doubtless somewhat through circumstances, but also out of personal conviction.
In the nineteenth century, Protestant missionary societies prolifer-
ated, but still on the fringe of Church organization. And it is precisely one of the aspects of the Church reawakening that in the
twentieth century the link between the mission and the Church is
increasingly preoccupying the minds of numerous Protestants. Thus
Churches on their organizational side have been led to try to arrange

a closer collaboration with missionary societies. Perhaps, indeed, by a kind of swing of the pendulum, one tendency in present-day Protestant theological thought is in danger of reaching an exaggeration complementary to the sixteenth-century one, namely, considering the Church purely and simply as a mission and thereby forgetting the fact that it is a community.

Finally, the sign of rebirth with which we shall conclude our enumeration is the awareness of the scandal inherent in existing divisions among Christians, and the accompanying gravitation towards ecumenicism.[3] To this we shall return later, for there is a basic bond between this aspect of the present-day rebirth of Protestantism and the renaissance of monastic or cenobitic life. But our intention at this moment is simply to give it the place which, because of its validity and importance, it deserves to occupy in this summary of the general traits of the contemporary Protestant revival.

Historically, then, despite efforts in the days of the Reformers to maintain or regain unity—and the feeling for unity on the part of people like, say, Bucer is well known—and despite continued efforts since that time—and they have been in fact more numerous than is generally supposed—still divisions among Christians multiplied and widened, especially in Reformation Churches. At the beginning of this century, certain responsible figures in the Protestant missionary world were sufficiently moved by this division, and by the paralyzing handicap which it placed upon evangelizers of the pagans, to seek effective measures for relief. This is where the ecumenical movement had its beginning. We cannot trace its history here, even briefly. Suffice it to say that after a period of getting on its feet the movement has taken a solid stance under the form of the World Council of Churches. But we must add, since this is sometimes forgotten, that the World Council does not represent the sum total of efforts for unity among Christians, or even among Protestants. Other efforts are also going on here and there to reachieve unity, or (more precisely from the Protestant viewpoint) to manifest a unity already realized in some mysterious, but not organic, way.

One more word deserves to be added. Ecumenical endeavors and

---

3 George Tavard, *Two Centuries of Ecumenism* (Fides, 1960; Mentor Omega, 1962) and Maurice Villain, *Unity: A History and Some Reflections* (Helicon, 1963) can be consulted for the facts of this development.

the restoration of the missionary orientation of the Church are not disconnected. The most striking sign of this fact was doubtless the merger in 1961, at Ceylon, of the International Council of Missions (made up of missionary societies) and the World Council of Churches (made up, as the name indicates, of Churches in the sociological sense of that term).

Now in the course of this general revival, Protestantism has also very noticeably evolved in its attitude towards Catholicism, and so much so that this point, it seems to us, ought not to be overlooked in the description of the context in which the renaissance of religious communities in Reformation Churches is taking place. It strikes us as correct to say that, not only on the individual, but also increasingly even on the Church level, Protestantism is coming to view Catholicism simultaneously as a heresy and as a challenge. In other words, it has become for Protestantism a concrete problem, solution of which is proving at once perplexing and rewarding. For this reason Protestants are following Catholic activities—especially missionary ones—with interest.

Even officially Catholicism is now the subject of a study which Protestantism is undertaking in a far from negative spirit. For instance, the Ecumenical Commission of the Protestant Federation of France has a special department for the study of French Catholicism. The *Vereinigte Evangelisch-Lutherische Kirche Deutschlands* has set up a theological commission on Catholicism. Moreover, the World Lutheran Federation is in the process of studying the formation of a committee for first-hand acquaintance with Catholicism on a world-wide scale. And the attitude towards this matter displayed at the general assembly of this organization, held in 1957 in Minneapolis, is decisive evidence of the quite positive position that many Protestants are taking in respect to the Roman Catholic Church today.

Such, then, is the context in which we must try to understand the facts set forth in the second part of this book. The rebirth of communities of regulars in Protestantism is taking place in a general climate of revival. Both on the theological and biblical level as well as on the more practical, concrete-life level of Protestant parishes and larger organizations, we live in a truly vibrant period of explorations, discoveries, new awarenesses, new achievements. Should we not add—reflecting the terms of the admonition *Ecclesia Catholica* of 1950, on the subject of efforts for unity—that the Holy Spirit is at work in the hearts of our Protestant brothers, and that in view of this spiritual impulse it will be most advantageous to hear the communities themselves on the justification of their birth and their existence in the heart of the Reformation Churches?

Chapter II

THE SIGNIFICANCE OF THE COMMUNITIES IN THE CHURCH AND IN THE WORLD

ONE of the fundamental reasons, as will be recalled, why the Reformation rejected the very principle of monasticism was the objection that it divided Christians into two categories: elite Christians on the one hand; ordinary Christians on the other. According to the Reformers, the "perfect" tended to grow increasingly uninterested in the rank and file of the Church. Bit by bit a separation, and even an opposition, between monks and Church tended to appear in the course of the historical development of monasticism. In other words, the Reformers had it that there was in the very nature of monasticism a leaven of separatism or of—to put it bluntly—schism.

Here we do not have either to justify or to counter the Reformers' criticism of the monasticism of their day. But this accusation of theirs has alerted present-day communities to the need of finding a way to make clear how they fit into the Church and into the world. They must, that is, show that they are not a potential seed of schism or separation in the body of the Church. Their intention is to be members of the Church, and to fulfil their duties in communion with and harmony with all the other members. The same impulse leads them to seek to exercise an authentically Christian presence in the world of men. For all, Christians or non-Christians, their intention is to be a sign.

Synthesis of the Communities and the Church

THE communities are members of the Church, the Body of Christ. This assurance, or rather requirement, may well first be considered here in the detailed words of the Apostle Paul:

117

> There are, of course, different kinds of gifts, though it is the same Spirit who gives them, just as there are different kinds of service, though it is the same Lord we serve, and different manifestations of power, though it is the same God who manifests his power everywhere in all of us. The revelation of the Spirit is imparted to each, to make the best advantage of it. One learns to speak with wisdom, by the power of the Spirit, another to speak with knowledge, with the same Spirit for his rule; one, through the same Spirit, is given faith; another, through the same Spirit, powers of healing; one can perform miracles, one can prophesy, another can test the spirit of the prophets; one can speak in different tongues, another can interpret the tongues; but all this is the work of one and the same Spirit, who distributes his gifts as he will to each severally.
>
> A man's body is all one, though it has a number of different organs; and all this multitude of organs goes to make up one body; so it is with Christ. We, too, all of us, have been baptized into a single body by the power of a single Spirit, Jews and Greeks, slaves and free men alike; we have all been given drink at a single source, the one Spirit. . . .
>
> And you are Christ's body, organs of it depending upon one another.[1]

What St. Paul says here of persons applies as well to communities and to parishes. In the Church there are different things to be done, and corresponding to these things, different talents. And, beyond argument, one thing from which Protestantism has suffered is having ground all of Christian life down to to the level of the parish. In fact, for centuries there was scarcely any place in the Reformation Churches for any function save the pastoral one. For a long time there were no Church organizations, no communities to take charge of certain activities which were nevertheless vital to the Church. As we saw in connection with the missions, for example, it was private societies, so to speak, which had to shoulder this responsibility. Not until the nineteenth century were certain service organizations (the deaconess movements) created in connection with the Church.

Against the leveling just spoken of, certain Christians have elected to react: the Gospel-patterned communities and the members of whom they are made up have sensed, in this matter, a requirement which the Lord places upon his Church. There are some duties which the parishes, for various reasons, cannot fulfil: and, to the problem of the fulfilment of some of these duties, communities of religious living together may be the answer.

---

1 1 Cor 12:4–13, 27.

The communities are particularly adapted for the ministry of re-treats. In fact furnishing a place and appropriate facilities for retreats is one of the inevitable features of all the foundations dealt with on previous pages here. For where are the desired silence, peace, and (at the same time) presence of fellow Christians to be found if not in these communities? Note well: the retreats which today are fast in-creasing in number in the world of fervent Protestants do not aim at alienating the retreatant from the workaday society to which he is accustomed. Quite to the contrary—and in this, too, the com-munities have a wise understanding of how the work of the Church is to be furthered—the aim is to make the retreatant better prepared to bear testimony as a Christian in his own customary surroundings. And the further aim is to prepare him to take his part in the Church, by giving him a superior spiritual training and causing him to under-stand in a still more personal way the Word that God has intended for him.

At any rate it is clear enough that the parishes are certainly not outfitted for this work, which is, however, by no means something eccentric or exceptional. In contrast, the communities, as just ex-plained in the foregoing paragraph, offer a setting of peace, of a meeting with God, which the bustle of modern-day life renders in-creasingly needful. Besides, there are the brothers, and the sisters, there, at the disposition of men or women in their spiritual quest, and to guard them from the perils of a too complete solitude. In this ministry, moreover, it will have to be admitted that the communities take up, or rather enlarge upon, the suggestion of Luther and others that such foundations might provide centers of spiritual and intel-lectual training for future pastors.

One man who has insisted very emphatically upon the necessity of co-ordination between communities and parishes is Walter Hümmer, founder of the *Christusbruderschaft* at Selbitz. In his opinion, they are mutually dependent. Without the community, or brotherhood, parishes are in danger of becoming a mere Christian association; conversely, without the parishes, a community tends to set itself up as a sect. Hümmer's assertions are open to discussion, of course, and we recognize the need of precaution against too easy generalizations. But what must not be overlooked in his contribution is that the liaison between the communities and the other organs of the Church,

9

most especially the parishes, must be an organic one, and that conversely the parishes, through this organic relationship, need the communities as radiant hearths of spiritual energy.

At Selbitz itself, it is worth noting, there is no view that the communities and parishes are but complementary arcs in the quadrant of Christian life. On the contrary, between the village parish here and the *Christusbruderschaft* there is a continuous vital interchange—in fact, a symbiosis of parish and community. The brothers are the pastor's chief co-operators in various ministrations (the young, the sick, etc.), while members of the congregation contribute in every possible material and spiritual way to the development and promotion of the brothers' community.

Apart from Selbitz, do the communities generally fulfil a ministry in the Church? They play a very important part, for example, in ecumenical endeavors. And here, again, is a new form of ministry which the parishes cannot themselves directly take care of, for the most part. Naturally, in nearly every Protestant faith are to be found specialists on the ecumenical question. But in addition to, and in co-ordination with, these there must be in every faith a spiritual ministry, for the need is to translate into concrete Christian life the mere utterances of theologians engaged in ecumenical studies and research, and—more important still—to translate into concrete life the unity already present in the mystery of Christ.

Similarly, the communities for the most part are places where Christians of different faiths meet. This is strikingly true of the Marienschwestern community at Darmstadt, for example, and even more so (though in a somewhat different way) of such communities as that of Taizé. Because of such meetings—the conversations thus made possible, and the fast friendships resulting—the communities may claim to fulfil a thoroughgoing ministry of reconciliation.

As just hinted, Taizé plays a very special part in this ministry. This we say not only because the brothers of this community have published a certain number of works which have contributed to bringing Christians into contact, and not only because certain brothers participate in the activities of the World Council of Churches and other ecumenical liaison groups, nor only because the brothers themselves belong to different Church branches and indeed to different faiths—but above all because in their essential spiritual life they have undertaken both to contemplate the tragedy of division and to nourish the hope of unity.

For the community and the individual brothers of Taizé, Christian unity is no mere object of theological study and speculation; nor is the quest for it but one activity among others, though one to which they feel particularly attached. No, Christian unity, we must go so far as to say, is their very life. Admittedly, this may not have been true from the community's first beginnings. It was the spiritual development of all the members which brought them to the point of accepting in their own persons the shame of Christian division and of the self-contradiction it implies, and at the same time of attempting to incarnate in their own persons what is already accomplished in Jesus Christ, but still on the way to realization on earth—unity among all Christians.

That ecumenicism is a call to meet a situation that cannot be put off is quite clear to the Taizé brothers themselves, as is the fact that it is a call to subject to a constant re-examination their conception of the Reformation, as witness these lines of Roger Schutz, their prior:

> This spiritual route of ecumenicism leads us near to the heart of the issues. We acquire a new conception of the Reformation, and of ourselves as its children. The Reformation no longer looks to us like a new Pentecost, inaugurating a new Church, but like a renovation produced by the Holy Spirit for the purification of the one, holy, universal, and apostolic Church. Of course what came out of this renovation in the way of schism, and constant debate, must be deplored; but if the Reformed can regain their positive prophetic mission in relationship to the Catholic Church, God will be able to turn the evil of division into good. The Reformation—which ought to have taken place on the inside of the Catholic Church—can penetrate it via the medium of charity, and succeed, not by demolishing it, but by causing those within it to recenter their attention on the essential treasures which it has always possessed. [2]

The first justification for the evangelical communities then, as we have just seen, is that in the life of the Church they must play a part which is indispensable, and which no one else can play, both on the level of the parish and on the level of the whole organization. Each

---

2 R. Schutz, "Résultats théologiques et spirituels des rencontres œcuméniques avec les catholiques romains," *Verbum Caro*, X (1956), p. 22.

in its own way, they are very well aware of this part, and recognize in it a proof that they face no real danger of "separatism."

In their synthesis with the Church, and in playing therein their exclusive part, the communities find themselves also face to face with the world of men. We must now see what part they aim to play in this world.

Synthesis of the Communities and the World

MONASTICISM has often been understood as a flight from the world. The first hermits took refuge in the desert solitudes to escape the dangers incurred in contacts with men. Doubtless many monks did feel that for them an existence among the masses of mankind endangered their spiritual life. That there was a kind of contradiction here the Reformers were quick to point out, perhaps forgetting that the following of Christ does involve some kind of rupture with the world.

How do the brothers and sisters of the Protestant communities of today react in the face of the world of men? In a way generally somewhat different from what one usually imagines the most genuine monastic or religious vocation to be, they aim to take an interest in the problems of modern-day human beings.

The foundation of these communities does not correspond, in fact, with any need to exhume the creations of the past in order to provide the pleasures of a historical restoration. The brothers and sisters of these communities are alive to the fact that our own day lays its hand upon all of us. It does not strike them as genuinely Christian to withdraw into a nostalgic remembrance of things past. Without the least disdain for the accomplishments of yesteryear, wrought among circumstances wholly different from our own, they believe in coming to grips with today's problems. In this, by the way, they come astonishingly close to just what, in their day, the founders of the great Catholic orders believed in doing.

Listen to what Max Thurian, in *Marriage and Celibacy*, had to say on the subject:

> The Christian life of celibates is lived in the history of men, and the more they risk being considered as living apart from real life, the more they are bound to share that life by being present to our time in a concrete way. The ethic, the existence of a celibate community must

not try to adapt an order of the past, but care must be taken that it have a meaning for other men in order to be up to date. To speak in psychological terms, a regular community ought not to consider itself as a collective *ego* at the heart of the Church. Nor should it be in the *third person*, as a reality placed in a situation, which can be spoken of and given a label, lives its life independently of others, irrespective of their reactions. For a regular community of Christian celibates to be in our time it must always be in the *second person*, an important and necessary element in the dialogue of men, always called upon and answering, always called in question and asking questions.

Celibates and their communities are opposed to all 'reaction.' On account of their freedom they refuse to become attached to systems and to memories. They are always on the march, seeking the most dynamic situation in the present time. They do not condemn social evolution, technical progress, or scientific or psychological discoveries. As far as is intellectually or practically possible for them they are always seeking afresh what man can and should be in our present time—not what he might be in a past or ideal situation—and how he can still remain a true man. They themselves wish to be such human beings. It is in this real and living existence that the Christian celibate will find his fulfill-ment.[3]

The actual way in which this presence in the world is realized in the various communities differs a great deal. One general tendency that may be noted, however, is the practice of sending brothers or sisters in groups of two or three into places where human conditions are particularly difficult. In fact, it appears that the best way to keep from isolating one's self from the problems of men is to take upon one's self the most painful distresses that are theirs today.

For the same reason, in several present-day communities the most frequent form of poverty selected is that which the poor of today actually suffer from—those who just manage to earn their daily bread by hard work. This experience is often accompanied, incidentally, by an increased awareness of the importance and the dignity of human labor. Work stops seeming a mere pastime, "busy work" that any other sort of activity might substitute for—some sort of play, really. No, work begins to assume, for brothers and sisters, the kind of importance it has for the general run of men: a difficult struggle of man against himself, but at the same time, the triumph of the human spirit over matter, for the good of all humankind; the painful way

3 Max Thurian, *Marriage and Celibacy* (London: SCM Press, 1959), pp. 120–121.

whereby man must make a livelihood, but, at the same time, the tie that binds man with men.

The necessity of contact with the world has still another side, however. If a Christian must be in contact with the world because he is, himself, *in* the world, he is nevertheless not *of* the world. The communities must live in the world, but without being of it. And this the brothers and sisters must express as well as their solidarity with the world. In fact, the very existence of these communities, their way of living, and their way of looking at life must be a challenge to the world, and, against the secularization which menaces Christendom, a living protest.

Our world today is menaced. On the one hand, it is in danger of being engulfed in a collectivism which denies the idea of a person, and of personal rights; and heaven knows that this protean menace is no bogy. On the other hand, it faces the opposite danger of falling —as a result of a pretended safeguarding of the rights of the human person—into the no lesser evil of individualism, itself finally just as destructive of personal values. Even in the Churches—and the pioneers of these communities are thinking here primarily of the Protestant faiths—individualism has been in the saddle for decades, spreading, from this vantage, death and destruction. These Christian communities, then, are trying to provide the concrete resolution of this basic problem: finding a form of common life which is not a destruction of the person, but on the contrary, something wherein the person can reach full expansion, and, at the same time, insuring to each his full self-realization without prejudice to the community of his fellows.

Moreover, our modern world, whether collectivist or individualist —doubtless sometimes both at once—is menaced by still other dangers. The greatest of these is perhaps the consequence of our substantial technical advances: modern man, having surrendered completely to a craving for well-being and for ease, has become mesmerized by comfort. Therefore—though without any basic opposition to progress, or disdain for the discoveries which have enabled man to tame the forces of nature and harness them for his profit—the brothers and sisters of these communities are alert to give public evidence, by their way of life, that the be-all and end-all of man does not consist of material riches and the manifold *things* that riches command, but a surpassing of one's self.

More generally, in a world which rests its security upon money, upon comfort, and upon what it calls knowing the angles, the communities proclaim the fact that there is no real security save in the faith and in a conscience that is free.

The Communities as a Sign

THUS we reach the fundamental *raison d'être* of communities in Christ's Church, as understood by these Protestant brothers and sisters: the community is first of all, and essentially, a *sign*. As Pastor Schutz puts it:

> A cenobitical community is a sign; its first task is not to preach, not to communicate words, not to engage in activities. Its first function is to exist as a sign, of the Church, and in the world. A sign is not something heard, nor is it a kind of dumb show. A sign is something that strikes us, and directs our attention towards the thing signified, which, in turn, has its way with us, producing the desirable impact upon us, and thus eliciting from us the necessary reactions.
>
> The community is a sign of *the coming kingdom*. By its common ownership of property, it prefigures the Kingdom's totality. By its requirement of celibacy, it prefigures the Kingdom as the plenitude of divine love, undiminished by particularity. . . . It is the Christian community raised to the nth power, extending as far as possible the requirements of total community.[4]

It seems that there are, in fact, three basic significances which the Protestant communities of our day are designed to bear:

a) By their very existence they are to be a sign of the coming Kingdom. In the face of a world secure in its own resources, and of a Church so long accustomed to not seeing Christ come again that many Christians have given up thinking that he will come, they announce that we have reached the last act of human history, and that the time is short. More portentously still, they proclaim to all that the coming of the Kingdom of God and its success will not be the same as the ultimate progress of this world, that in fact the approaching Kingdom will break with our departing world. Thus the com-

---

4 R. Schutz, "Naissance de communautés dans les églises de la Réforme," *Verbum Caro,* X (1955), No. 33.

munities, standing as it were where time itself must have a stop, prophetically dramatize the termination of the ages.

b) It is indisputably clear that Christians are prone to take Christ's words with a grain of salt, and to feel that their vocation as Christians is only one thing to be taken into consideration along with a good many others. Now the communities, as a sign of the Kingdom's break with the world and its way of thinking, concretely manifest that the requirements Christ lays upon Christians do not depend upon this, that, and the other thing, but are absolute. This the communities do by taking absolutely seriously their own commitments of poverty, celibacy, and obedience (if, in the case of some communities, not "commitments," then fundamental necessities of their common-life organization).

Take celibacy. If it is an adumbration of the coming Kingdom, in which there will no longer be any marrying and giving in marriage— any conjugal relations—as Christ himself declared, it is also a sign that here and now Christ will be enough for Christians, and that for his sake they dare give up anything and everything else. At the same time it is a concrete sign—set up in a world where the only emperor is sex—that marriage is far from a human necessity laid upon everybody, but itself a special call from God. Thus does the vocation to Christian celibacy, paradoxically if you will, make clearer the call to sanctification of marriage. The brothers and sisters themselves emphasize the fact that they, in their lives as celibates, have a significance for married Christians. Max Thurian writes:

> When the call to celibacy is too little heard, marriage gradually comes to be thought of as a reality of the purely natural order. . . . One of the first results of Christian celibacy and not the least important, is the revaluation of marriage as a way of life willed by God for the service of Christ and the Church.[5]

Similarly, the renouncement of private property in favor of common ownership is a sign of the Kingdom; but it is also a sign for Christians here and now, incessantly tempted as they are to rest their security upon wealth and to make property rights sovereign. Christ exacts from all the renouncement of this kind of material security, and certain confidence that our necessary bread will be given us each day in accordance with his promise.

5 Thurian, p. 44.

c) Finally, the communities are a sign of the Christian community which is the Church—a small-scale model of the Church, so to speak, wherein the whole can be seen in small compass, or perhaps a kind of prototype. Pastor Schutz, prior of Taizé, was remarking already in the first days of the community that a resident community of that kind

> recalls to the passer-by the principles of the Christian community when carried to their logical conclusion. The preaching of the word must always be completed by this kind of preaching by example. As that kind of example, the resident community can provide, in the Church, an image of the Christian community—an image clear, sharp-cut, and in its particularity especially capable of producing an effect on the individualistic sensibilities of our day.[6]

A religious community provides a bird's-eye view of the ideal Christian world, of course, because the spirit which presides over the existence of a fraternal community includes a concrete gift of self, a keeping of one's self as approachable and as free and as ready to serve other members as if they were Christ himself; now these are obviously the essential characteristics of charity, which is the very spirit of the whole Church. As regards charity, then, the communities exhibit the feeling that should exist among all members of the Body of Christ. And as regards faith, they render a similar service: they are a concrete expression of the fact that not all sides of the Gospel are to be seen except in a "community"—that we can understand (and live by) the Gospel only if we do so as a body: the Body, that is, of Christ.

Again, the communities are an image of the Church through the diversity of functions fulfilled there by means of the unity of the whole: every brother or every sister has his exact function in the whole, and he fulfils it in the name of all, at the same time recognizing and respecting the value of each of the other functions which are complementary to his own.

Thus at the conclusion of this chapter we come again to the idea of a body composed of many organs: as it is in the organization of the Church, so is it, the communities believe, in their own organization—unity in functional variety.

6 R. Schutz, *Introduction à la vie communautaire* (Geneva: Labor et Fides, 1944), pp. 28-29.

By the same token, the first answer that these communities can give in face of possible criticism, is this: In the Church there are a variety of functions; of these functions the communities fulfil some that no other Church institutions could. And this duty within the Church, and the communities' consciousness of this duty, do not preclude their being present in the world, of having a message for the world, and—more important still—of being for the world both a sign of the presence of Christ and a dramatized prophecy of his daily—imminent—return.

Chapter III

VOCATION, BASIS OF COMMUNITY LIFE

THE answer given by Protestant religious communities to the objection that monasticism by its very nature introduces a source of division into the Church is doubtless valid. (What that answer is we have seen in the chapter immediately preceding.) And, true enough, such an answer has not only the negative force of destroying the objection to religious life in its relationship with the Church, but also the positive force of establishing the fact that resident communities have a part that must be played in the complex Body which is the Church. Nevertheless, by itself this answer would not suffice to justify the foundation of these communities.

If we really wish to understand the basic reasons why such communities were founded and why they continue to exist, in Protestantism, we must understand that the brothers and sisters in these communities justify their form of life primarily in terms of *vocation*.

In the first part of this book we directed the attention of the reader to Bucer's use, in the sixteenth century, of this idea of vocation in connection with celibacy. In our own day, this same idea is clearly the central point in the reasoning whereby the communities explain their form of life and establish, specifically, the validity both of the commitments which the brothers and sisters make and of the definitive nature of these commitments as generally understood.

Two Forms of Evangelical Vocation

IN the average Protestant mind, supported by an uncompromising adherence to the opinion of the Reformers, there is only one form of Christian life possible. A Christian is in the world, and it is there that he must make the Gospel his life. He must do so in his family life, his professional life, his civic life, and so on—without seeking any special, transcendent "service of God" anywhere else.

This one-line conception of Christian life entails, as everyone knows, very exacting rules for everyday human behavior; and not without reason has the austerity of numerous Protestant homes attracted attention. The concrete realities of human life, one's duties at work, one's duties as a citizen—all this is taken with the utmost seriousness because it is precisely in this line that one's vocation as a Christian achieves its specific realization.

Nevertheless, if this one-line view of a Christian's calling finds solid justification in the writings of the Reformers, it is not so easily justified in terms of what we find in the New Testament. Attention to but a few passages there can serve to alter that view appreciably. And it is primarily from this latter point of view that the reasoning of present-day community members on this subject must be understood.

It must be noticed first of all that in the New Testament are found two distinct types of Christian community. On the one hand, the Jerusalem community, the original cell of Christianity, practiced common ownership of property and required of its members, it appears, a change from the ground up in their way of life.

> They occupied themselves continually with the apostles' teaching, their fellowship in the breaking of the bread, and the fixed times of prayer; and every soul was struck with awe, so many were the wonders and signs performed by the apostles in Jerusalem. All the faithful held together, and shared all they had, selling their possessions and their means of livelihood, so as to distribute to all, as each had need. They persevered with one accord, day by day, in the Temple worship, and, as they broke bread in this house or that, took their share of food with gladness and simplicity of heart, praising God, and winning favor with all the people. And each day the Lord added, to their fellowship, those who were to be saved.[1]

But on the other hand there also existed, in the various cities where the preaching of Paul or other apostles had found a response, Churches which in their concrete life seem to have been quite different from the mother Church at Jerusalem. At Corinth, for example, Paul

---

1 Acts 2: 42–47.

did not require a common ownership of property. After their conversion and reception into the Christian community, these Christians led a concrete life quite like the one they had led previously, even though the spirit of that life had now radically changed.

Of course, when it comes to the New Testament, we cannot make out so clear a classification as that today between parishes and stable communities. Nor should the New Testament texts on this subject be made to seem more informative than they actually are. But they are not so cryptic that we cannot discern that the contracting of Christian life to the single form of parish life (on the plan of Corinth and elsewhere) cannot have cited, in its favor, what the primitive Church originally experienced. On the contrary, it is with full right that twentieth-century Protestant communities cite the precedent of the Jerusalem community, as nearly all their predecessors—Catholics in centuries past, Anglicans in the last century—have cited it. Present-day Protestant communities have undertaken to realize the plan of Christian life followed at Jerusalem in the very first days of the Church.

In addition, a certain number of Gospel passages express—quite clearly, in the view of the brothers and sisters of these communities— the existence of a call from God to the original form of Christian life. The way in which Calvin, for example, understood Christ's bid to the rich young man—"If thou hast a mind to be perfect, go home and sell all that belongs to thee; give it to the poor, and so the treasure thou hast shall be in heaven; then come back and follow me"[2]—has little in common with the directions which community members understand these words of Christ to contain. For Calvin, Christ's rejoinder to the young man's statement was intended for the young man alone, to make him aware that in contrast with his own account of his situation he was leagues removed from a perfect keeping of the law.

The young man, in other ways not bad at heart, was presumptuous; and he replied that he had kept all the commandments since childhood. But it is quite clear that he had a long way to go to reach the point he prided himself upon having attained. Now if the young man was to learn how little he had profited by the justice he boasted of having encompassed, the vice hidden in his heart would have to be uncovered; for, being rich, he had an unconscious affection for riches. That was why, since he

2 Mt 19: 21.

himself did not feel it, Jesus Christ had to probe the sore spot by suggesting that he sell all his possessions. . . . Those of us who allege this text as validating the monastic state make the mistake of generalizing a doctrinal principle from a particular case.[3]

In present-day commentaries on this text, above all in the significance for religious life that Protestant communities are led to find there, they insist much more on the eschatological sense of Christ's supposition: "If you have a mind to be perfect": the subject here is not a Christian's saintly behavior, but his very mode of existence.

Some, in fact, must signify Christ's presence in the world at all times and in all the circumstances and conditions that flesh is heir to. But others, like the young man, must be a sign by their very way of life that we are living in the last age, and that we must be hastening towards the end, the conclusion, the final goal. And precisely in order to be an eschatological sign, this original Christian life must be pursued in a kind of secession from the values of the temporal order: wealth, family, independence.

Christ's appeal to renounce marriage "for the sake of the Kingdom" is still more specific. In the face of the requirements of marriage as Christ presented them to the Pharisees who had come to catechize him on the subject—the necessity of fidelity based on the indissolubility of the marriage bond—the disciples were not a little disconcerted, and were brought to remark, "If the case stand so between man and wife, it is better not to marry at all." Christ first answered that an understanding of what he had just said, and was about to say, concerning marriage was not given to everyone, "but only by those who have the gift." For Thurian, and for others with him, what must be understood here is that

> if there are Christians to whom it is given to understand the exacting saying of Jesus concerning marriage and to obey this vocation to marital union, there are others who are able to hear the call to celibacy and who must understand it and respond to it. 'He that is able to receive it, let him receive it,' says Jesus.[4]

Otherwise put, there are here indicated the two possible vocations: one vocation, exacting and difficult, to indissoluble marriage; another vocation, also exacting and difficult, to celibacy. And as for

---

3 Calvin, *Institution chrétienne*, 1559, IV, iii, pp. 256–257.
4 Max Thurian, p. 44.

the latter one, Christ is distinguishing here, among several material possibilities, the one which truly corresponds to the conditions of a vocation: the question is not of a physical deformation, whether congenital or effected by surgery, but of a spiritual orientation: celibacy in this case is undertaken "for the sake of the Kingdom."

Finally, the possibility of Christian celibacy is recognized explicitly by St. Paul, in the First Epistle to the Corinthians. Calvin, of course, in his commentary on the verses in question, did recognize celibacy as a possibility. But he thought it something extremely rare; and we have seen that, in harmony with the other Reformers, he did not think that a commitment to this way of life could be acceptable to a Christian.

Members of communities find a less restricted meaning in these verses. In their view, Paul first of all accepts marriage unreservedly, going so far as to recommend it in cases where celibate life results in the heat of passion; in this case, that is, it is better to marry. All the same, if we read what the man actually says, Paul declares his preference for celibacy: if to marry is better than to experience the heat of passion, not to marry is better still—on condition, of course, that one can live as a celibate without licentiousness.

The reason for this preference Paul furnishes by pointing out that a person who is married is required to take an interest in the things of the world, whereas one who is not married is freer to take an active interest in the things that belong to God. Moreover, the Apostle sets this question in the context of a Christian's spiritual life, a matter which is not bound up with Paul's personal opinion that the end of the world was close in time.

For St. Paul, the time was short; the fabric of this great globe was due to dissolve. Since our minutes were hastening to their end, it was better to press forward with such intensity that each individual could turn his back on the world for the last time and cast in his lot with God. Do we not find here again, in a different context, the idea that celibacy is an eschatological sign? Better to remain unmarried, because the time was short.

And yet this was not a surrender to everyone's free choice in the matter, as if everyone was to decide upon his own spiritual orientation: "Each of us has his own endowment from God," St. Paul explained, "one to live in this way, another in that."[5] It was a question, therefore, of a gift from God, and therefore also of a vocation; one person received one, another another. And though St. Paul was grateful for having, himself, received the vocation to celibacy, and appreciated all its advantages "for the sake of the Kingdom," nevertheless he could not impose it on someone else: for it was not up to him, but to the Lord, to accord this gift and vocation to some, and not to others. Nor did he give any command here, but "my opinion, as one who is, under the Lord's mercy, a true counselor."[6]

Gift of celibacy, vocation to celibacy, possibility—more generally —of a way of Christian life which breaks with even the legitimate goods the use of which still permits one to die to one's self and live for God in Christ—such are the elements which members of Protestant religious communities in our day find in their fresh reading of the New Testament. Moreover, for them, this vocation and this gift entail one characteristic which the Reformation rejected explicitly: irrevocability. To this we shall now give closer attention.

Vocation and Commitment

WHAT must first be noted is that a vocation, whether to marriage or to consecrated celibacy, is a Christian absolute, which affects "the whole of one's being" and has no validity save in a surpassing of "our whole being on account of the call we have received."[7] If there is a real vocation, then there must be an absolute requirement imposed by Christ—without whose gift, of course, the requirement could not be met. And since Christ does not, so to speak, half call us, or call us but for a time, and since, similarly, he does not repent of his gifts, then man's response—again, a result of this gift—cannot be other than total, absolute, definitive.

In the gospel text referred to a few pages back, the very expression used by Christ in reference to those who are celibates "for the sake of the Kingdom" expresses the permanent character of their state: they have made themselves "eunuchs," and in this regard Christ compares their case to that of "eunuchs who were so born from the

---

5 1 Cor 7:7.
6 1 Cor 7:25.
7 R. Schutz, "Introduction" to Max Thurian, *Marriage and Celibacy*, pp. 15, 16.

mother's womb" and of "eunuchs who were made so by men." In these last two cases the definitive character is beyond question, surely? It seems to be precisely this characteristic of finality that Christ is emphasizing in employing the same word to designate those who renounce marriage for the sake of the Kingdom. Max Thurian writes:

> This word must imply some aspect of the reality which he is describing. It was needed to make them understand that the condition of celibates for the Kingdom of Heaven's sake possesses an irrevocable character; in this way of life there can be no turning back. Like those who cannot marry for physical reasons, the celibates of the Spirit permanently give up marriage and sexual life.[8]

In this regard—and contrary to what the Reformers repeatedly maintained—celibacy and marriage are characterized in the same way. In consequence of various circumstances, the Reformers—except Bucer—did see that marriage is irrevocable. Curiously, they did not grant the same quality to celibacy for the Kingdom of Heaven. They did not perceive—or perhaps even, like Luther, in certain cases they did not wish to perceive—that the objections they made against the definitive character of the celibacy of monks or priests could be applied also to marriage.

We must also note that denying the permanency of celibacy for the sake of the Kingdom ended up in a denial of the possibility of celibacy itself. If celibacy was not permanent, why, it was no different from the temporary period before marriage: it lost its specific character. There was then, in very truth, nothing new in it; and what one granted in admitting the possibility of a vocation to celibacy one took back in denying it a permanent and absolute character.

What is said here of celibacy is also to be said of the other necessary conditions for the "religious life." Vocation and endowment from God call for, in man, a commitment as absolute as the call itself: we can, after all, attribute nothing "half baked" to God.

May we direct attention to the fact that celibacy for the sake of the Kingdom of God is not a life led in solitude (at least in the situations we are dealing with here). The celibate has brothers and sisters, who live as a community; and it would be a mistake to attempt to examine, out of this perspective of community, the various elements

---

8 Thurian, p. 56.

10

of the vocation: celibacy, common ownership of property, and obedience. And it would be just as much a mistake to try to see the permanent character of the commitment out of this perspective.

A religious community, in fact, cannot be compared to an association freely entered into by those in agreement with its ends and its means, and as freely withdrawn from when the members are no longer in agreement upon these. No, from such groups—even though religious, and even Christian—a religious community is distinguished by the fact that men enter there in order to realize a particular form of Christian life to which they believe themselves called by vocation and which must absorb the whole of their being. They enter there in order to realize this form of life together, because they think that the Gospel cannot be lived in its fulness except in concrete fraternal communion. They therefore require of one another an equal willingness for fraternal communion. If their purpose there is to live according to certain commitments which they believe absolute, then they feel it is not too much to ask of their brothers the same intention. Seen in this light, fraternal communion would be but a mutual illusion, and would be radically compromised, if each one did not give to the others what he himself expects and exacts of them.

Of course one could imagine—indeed they exist—certain temporary associations, created, for example, for some special purpose. But then there would be no question of the members' realizing in it a *vocation* equal and similar to that of marriage, but only of serving a certain amount of time in Church work, with the expectation of resuming one's habitual style of life afterwards. Certainly such associations would not necessarily require common ownership of property, or celibacy; and obedience there would be meaningless except in connection with the determinate and limited purpose which the association was created to achieve.

Religious communities properly so called have none of those limiting factors. In a sense, they are all-absorbing entities precisely because their members feel that by entering them they are responding to a *vocation*, and to the gift which matches it, just as a Christian man or wife feels that he is responding to a particular vocation when contracting marriage.

Thus a community requires of its members the irrevocable decision to progress together towards Christ for the whole of their lives or, more precisely, until (to resume here the eschatological implications of community life) the return of Christ. The three commitments—celibacy, common ownership of property, and obedience—both express and realize this decision. If, in fact, people undertake to form a community, and to find in it their particular choice of life, it is quite necessary that the renouncement of marriage be permanent, that common ownership be absolute and absorb in an "ours" both "mine" and "thine," and that, finally, each member accept in advance both his place and others' places in the community and consent to integrate his own activities into the common endeavor—that is, that he recognize above himself, as above the others, the authority of the community, which it expresses either through a single member —the superior or prior—or through several, and ultimately through the totality of the brothers or sisters.

To be sure, so as to safeguard the idea of God's transcendence and of his liberty, Protestantism generally rejects the idea of so specific a vocation, or, even conceding such an idea, customarily will not grant that such a vocation can become concretely and visibly manifest in a permanent commitment. In thus championing the liberty of God, average Protestantism seeks also to champion the liberty of man.

In reply, members of the communities generally make this preliminary remark: this liberty of the Spirit is not invoked to turn marriage into a purely temporary arrangement; it is therefore not logical to invoke it in connection with celibacy undertaken for the sake of the Kingdom, and in connection with the religious life. If the commitment to marriage can be definitive and irrevocable with no disparagement of liberty, it is not easy to see why a similar commitment to religious community life must imply any such disparagement.

But the matter cannot rest there. More fundamentally, in the problem here, it is the significance of the Incarnation, and of the presence, since Pentecost, of the Holy Spirit in each individual believer that must be emphasized. Thurian writes:

> The difficulty, which will always create in the Church and in the Christian life an inevitable and salutary tension, is to maintain together the rights of event and of institution, of reformation and of succession, of newness and of continuity, of liberty and of faithfulness. Only the Church which can accommodate in its existence a prophetic and reforming renewal within an institution which is catholic (the term is used here in the sense of the unity and the totality of the Church in time and

space) and apostolic (i.e. bound to its origins) can manifest in its being both the liberty and the faithfulness of God. Similarly in the Christian life there is no true inner liberty, that is, liberty guided by the Holy Spirit, without a firm resolution and discipline in obedience to the Lord. Once we reject the possibility that God commits himself together with the Christian in decisions which involve a definitive character and which are expressed socially, we are in danger of losing the true idea of Christian liberty. . . .

But, some will say Christian liberty understood in the ordinary Protestant sense is not an anarchical liberty, but rather the possibility of remaining open and available to the orders of the Word of God. Here again, it is a misunderstanding of the liberty of God to believe that he cannot declare a definitive Word on a person. It is the final refusal to see that in Christ actual promises are made to us which will be fulfilled. But, some will add, it is legitimate to believe that God, in his mysterious plan, has decided that a man should remain unmarried in order to serve him; but it is not possible for that man to commit himself permanently; he ought to remain in a state of waiting and dependence. We realize here to what extent this way of thinking is bound to a religion which is still characterized by Old Testament piety and which has not fully appropriated the result of the Incarnation: that Christ still has his human expression in his Church today. This conception also shows that the mystery of Pentecost has not really been understood: that the Holy Spirit, shed abroad in the Church and in the hearts of men, makes each Christian a temple of the Spirit of God.[9]

Otherwise put, in a commitment which a man makes, God commits himself with him—or, better, this man's concrete commitment translates and expresses God's commitment. Real Christian liberty is not thereby destroyed or compromised; quite to the contrary. For the question is not of an anarchic liberty, little different from caprice or arbitrariness, but of a liberation from sin and from the Law, through the operation of Christ. This liberation introduces the Christian, through the merits of Christ, into a new life of obedience and fidelity to God's requirements. And vocation, which as we have seen is a gift, is also a requirement for the one who receives it. He is simply recognizing the fact in responding to that vocation by his commitment to God's own commitment.

The Rule and the Interior Disciplines

ONE problem, however, remains: If true Christian liberty is not compromised by the commitment made in response to a vocation recog-

9 Thurian, pp. 97–98.

nized as coming from the Lord, will this liberty not then be lost by submission to a rule and to uniform prescriptions given the community? Is there not, in applying to one's individual self these community enactments, some danger of falling into a certain formalism? Finally, will the community member not be led to find in the accomplishment of these prescribed activities the essential part of his spiritual life?

That there are entailed in the rule, and in the community disciplines, and in the practices of asceticism, some real risks—this no one would think of denying; but it may be pointed out that there is, in fact, no form of Christian life which does not entail, necessarily, some risks, and that no one is absolutely insured against confusing, in practice, the essentials of Christian life with the concrete ways in which these essentials must be put into practice. Nevertheless, in Christian life of any kind it is wholly necessary to translate one's faith into concrete activities. For Christianity is not merely a theoretical adherence to Christ, much less a religious dilettantism. It is obedience to the word of God and to his commands.

Of course, any time that spiritual discipline, mortification, and pious activity do not spring from faith, the result we can expect is a formalistic falsification of Christianity, even though perhaps not betrayed by any visible lack of genuinity. To each of its members the community ought to be a help against this danger. But it should also call upon each to keep from drowsing off into a religious quietude which is just as destructive of true Christian life as a formalistic activism is.

The goal, after all, is each member's converting his whole being into an instrument of service to Christ and to his brothers. There is no question here of asceticism for the sake of asceticism, of a self-mastery finding its ultimate reason for being and its justification in self-admiration. In Christianity there can never be any question of a moral perfection for moral perfection's sake. Yet, when all this has been granted, it remains strictly true that the whole of man, man in all his humanity, must undergo a rigorous discipline in order to be able to render better service and to remain plastic in every regard to the operation of the Lord and of his Spirit. In other words, the goal is for each member to place under the domain of Christ his every thought, word, and deed—to realize the ideal proposed to Christians by St. Paul: to do all for Christ Jesus.

Here is where the interior disciplines and ascesis must come into play. And since the brothers and sisters of the communities we are discussing have decided to travel together towards Jesus Christ, this discipline and this ascesis will be undergone in common, the pilgrims bearing one another's burdens, to fulfil the law of Christ. To such guarantees against perfectionism and other self-deception, community life joins, in addition, a daily invitation to the fervor of the Spirit.

We believe that this explanation renders faithfully these communities' and their members' position as regards the need of a community asceticism and interior disciplines. Certain communities go even further, and believe, in addition, in the necessity of a rule. Actually, fundamentally the same reasons argue in favor of a rule, though with a generally greater emphasis on the unity to be hoped for from recognition of a rule uniformly accepted.

It is moreover quite evident that at the stage of evolution which these communities have reached at present, their rule—when they have one—is modest and limited. It is ordinarily at the end of years of thought, and with every possible protection against a spirit of stampede, that a few principles of direction are adopted as a common rule, with the aim of making the Gospel ideal more personal with each member, to give it concrete shape for the particular community and its members, but also to insure to these members—always more or less in danger of an abatement of zeal despite frequent initial enthusiasm—certain permanent practical orientations possessing in some degree an independent worth.

This is no call, then, to view the rule as a kind of new law, the observance of which would by itself be a source of salvation. In the same way, neither are the disciplines or the ascetic practices, in the eyes of the brothers and sisters, "means" of salvation. They are well aware, and they often emphasize, that their justification and their sanctification derive to them from the activity of Christ himself. Rule, disciplines, ascetic practices—these are, for them, works of faith which spring from their commitment to the service of Christ and of their fellow man, and concretely constitute the spirit of their community.

Synthesis of Celibacy and Marriage

YET one last problem presents itself: that of the connection between a "religious" vocation and the Christian vocation "in the world." (We are well aware that, unfortunately, "in the world" is not a very happy expression, having, as it does, a more or less pejorative connotation; it is simply in want of a better that we use it here to denote the life of Christians who in accordance with their vocation enter into marriage and assume duties which are directly "secular.") How do the brothers and sisters think of their own life as Christians in relationship to the life of Christians "in the world" and in relationship to marriage? More specifically, do they think that celibacy and the religious life are in themselves superior to a Christian career "in the world," and to marriage? Or do they think that the two ways of life are of equal value?

The first thing to recall, in considering this matter, is that marriage and celibacy both correspond to a vocation to which are attached its own specific gifts and which requires of the person called an absolute commitment. In these regards, marriage and celibacy are to be thought of as of equal value.

Furthermore, they both have a distinctly religious significance. Marriage gives concrete expression to the fact that Christian life embraces all things human, because Christ sanctified them all by his incarnation. It is therefore part of the scheme wherein God is present to men in all the concrete realities of their existence. It also witnesses the fact that the order of nature was not destroyed by the coming of Christ and by the redemption, but contrariwise, received from these a new dignity.

Celibacy, in contrast, is a symbol of the break which, nevertheless, also exists between the order of nature and the order of the redemption: the triumph of the Kingdom of God is precisely not identical with the triumph of this world. Whoever wishes to follow Christ must choose him instead of everything else; and this choice of Christ instead of anything else, and Christ's *de facto* transcendence of all things else, are signified by marriage renounced for the sake of the Kingdom.

Now, at the same time, Chapter VII of the First Epistle to the Corinthians speaks of a superiority possessed by celibacy over marriage; given the possibility of the two, St. Paul thinks it better to remain celibate. How is this to be understood?

Many Protestant theologians will point out first of all that St. Paul is speaking of particular circumstances, and not in general; he says that this is the best counsel *"in times of stress."*

The communities, on the other hand, without denying the circumstantial reasons attached to St. Paul's statement about celibacy, prefer to emphasize the practical reasons also given explicitly by the Apostle. Whoever is a celibate is more free; he is better able to take time for the things of God. Not being obliged to busy himself with things of the world he may, in fact, devote his time to being "intent on holiness, bodily and spiritual." He can "attend on the Lord without distraction."

Concern with the claims of the Lord, concern with means of pleasing the Lord, these are the two advantages St. Paul attributes to celibacy. Yet these two advantages do not put the celibate in a superior position as regards salvation. This is a point which seems of capital importance to Protestant community-members. For salvation lies, not in works, but in faith, and community activities therefore have no direct influence on salvation. And, from this point of view, one can understand why some of them think this question, "marriage or celibacy," of but secondary importance. Furthermore, since in Christian marriage as well as in celibacy a Christian undertakes to respond to a divine call, there is no more obedience to God in the one case than in the other. As regards submission to the will of God, then, marriage and celibacy are objectively on the same level.

Greater practical advantage for the service of fellow man and for cultivation of the interior life: yes, this the brothers and sisters of the communities attribute to celibacy. A better spiritual or religious situation in the eyes of God: this they refuse to see in it. The unmarried and the married, it makes no difference, both are *committed* in response to a call and by fidelity to the concrete requirements which God places upon them. As Thurian puts it:

> So in the sight of God and in relation to salvation and obedience, marriage and celibacy are two equally valid ways of life, although they involve different values and meanings. However, in relation to the ministry and the contemplative life, celibacy is to be considered as a more favorable situation. . . . It is not superior or even more advan-

tageous, still less more meritorious, from the spiritual or moral point of view, to be a minister rather than a workman. Both vocations are equal in the sight of God. Still, it is obvious that the pastoral vocation is preferable from the point of the view of the Kingdom of God and the meditation of his Word. Objectively speaking, a minister ought to do more for the Church than a workman, and he has more time for contemplation. It is in this that the practical and interior value, not a spiritual or moral value, of the pastoral ministry lies. So it is with celibacy. . . .[10]

By the same token, a person who has a vocation to celibacy and, because of that vocation and a desire to submit himself to God's will regarding him, pledges himself permanently to membership in a celibate community must take great care not to succumb to pride and complacency. If, thanks to his state, he is more free, better situated for service of the Kingdom and for meditation of the Word, he is not thereby freed from himself, nor from the greatest spiritual perils. He has not been placed in a situation morally or spiritually superior to that of married Christians, nor dare he look patronizingly upon them.

Celibate Christians are necessary to married Christians as their complements in the organic Body of Christ; but the converse is equally true. Those who are celibate for the sake of the Kingdom equally need those committed by vocation to the state of marriage, for the former certainly do not, all by themselves, make up the Body of Christ. Nor are they even a spiritual elite in that Body, where each member serves the function for which he has been designated by his vocation, in harmony with the whole and respect for each of the other members and for their function.

---

10 Thurian, pp. 83–84.

Chapter IV

COMMUNITIES AND PROTESTANTISM:
KARL BARTH'S OPINIONS

WE have just seen how the members of Protestant religious communities (especially the theologians among them) justify the existence
of these communities, their principal characteristics, and, especially,
the commitments made to this way of life. Often enough, however,
when he takes a straight look at one or another of these communities,
an observer may wonder whether he is seeing something really
Protestant or not. Obviously this doubt is very natural on the part
of the average Protestant, who is far from accustomed to finding
convents and monks in his Church. But it is natural, too, on the part
of the average Catholic, who is accustomed to think of such things
as his Church's exclusive possession.

The answer to this question is extremely delicate. How, simply,
can we tell whether such and such a thing is or is not a genuine part
of an intellectual movement and a religious mentality such as Protestantism? At the very least, we should first have to define Protestantism—and that would be impossibility enough.

But try to give some answer to this question we must. What shall
we do? May we not suggest that it would be possible, in this matter,
to determine the opinions of someone who is unquestionably a rep-
resentative of Protestant theology? Of course, we hasten to add, we
are well aware that no Protestant theologian has such doctrinal
authority in his Church that what he says and writes will be recognized as correct, as truth, by all his coreligionists. Yet it does seem
to us that a theologian whose adherence to the Reformation and to
Reformation theology is beyond question would be just the man to
help settle our problem.

144

It is therefore to Karl Barth that we shall turn in order to inquire whether monasticism and religious life in the form we find them today in a certain number of Protestant communities may be considered "Protestant," or whether, on the contrary, they are currents of life and thought absolutely unacceptable to Churches originating in the Reformation.

In Volume III of his monumental work, *Kirchliche Dogmatik*, Karl Barth has occasion to raise now and again a certain number of problems concerning religious or monastic life, and of celibacy for the sake of the Kingdom as one of its aspects.

For him, the fundamental question is to determine whether the Reformation was strictly in accord with the New Testament on this point.

With growing assurance—but also from a single viewpoint—Luther attributed to work in the fields, in the shop, or in the family household the value of a "service of God," which had been attributed in his day to the activities of the cloister. Luther's point was doubtless of very great importance. But did not Protestantism then and in the centuries to follow insist upon this point too much? Did it not overrate marriage at the expense of celibacy? How far can the Word of God be brought to justify this preference? . . . Paul himself, in the perspective of the Lord's return, to correspond with the service required by the Lord in his spiritual army, understood celibacy as a call from God, and even gave all Christians the unequivocal advice that they should do as he did, for the Kingdom of Heaven.[1]

Christ's statement, reported by Matthew and Mark, on voluntary continence ("some are eunuchs who have made themselves such for the sake of the Kingdom of Heaven") has suggested to the Basle theologian still clearer conclusions:

These words do not imply an institution, or special state, of celibacy; they refer rather to individual decisions in the direction of celibacy. There is above all no question of a higher state of life to be occupied by celibates; but it is clearly indicated that there are individual situations which make decisions in this direction possible and indispensable. Therefore, for certain men, marriage is not only not required, but in fact forbidden for a limited time or permanently.

Nor, in light of these words, may it be claimed that marriage is in general and for everyone the higher way, the better decision. It is simply indicated that these latter days may now move a man to remain celibate,

---

1 Karl Barth, *Kirchliche Dogmatik*, III, iv, pp. 540–541.

so as to witness thus the relationship which exists between Christ and his Church.[2]

The words of St. Paul (Eph 5: 23), "Yes, these words are a high mystery, and I am applying them here to Christ and his Church," also lead Karl Barth to emphasize that marriage takes on, in the New Testament, a new dignity, one which supposes, besides it, another possibility.

It is striking that the word *gamos* only describes marriage once in the New Testament—"marriage is honorable in all" (Heb 13: 4). Elsewhere this word means a wedding and nearly always the eschatological wedding feast of Christ, the Bridegroom. . . . Precisely because marriage is no longer an *obligation* in the Church of the New Testament period the unmarried state is not a subject for shame and grief. On the contrary —and this is the other, positive aspect—when marriage received this new meaning and consecration, then it also became possible to understand and to value the *renunciation* of marriage as a possibility, a way, a matter of a particular gift and call.

It is an unquestionable fact—over which Protestant ethics has passed rather too lightly in the partiality for marriage that has developed in the struggle against the Roman celibacy of the priesthood and orders— that *Jesus Christ* himself, of whose true humanity there can be no doubt, had, apart from his Church, no other loved one, no other bride or wife, no other family, no other home.[3]

From this it clearly appears that for a Protestant theologian like Karl Barth, scarcely open to suspicion of Catholicizing tendencies, there really exists a *vocation* to celibacy, as there does a vocation to marriage. Of course, in the passages we have cited, Barth does not show himself favorable to an "institutionalization" of celibacy for the sake of the Kingdom. This at any rate does not seem to him indicated in the biblical verses he is citing. Above all is he opposed to the idea of the celibate state's superiority over the marriage state. But, this reservation once established, he freely admits—and not as something exceptional, almost hypothetical, as with the greater part of the Reformers—that a Christian may continue in celibacy for the sake of the Kingdom, not only for a time, but permanently, and may therefore renounce marriage.

2 *Ibid.*, p. 160, from the French translation and citation by Thurian, *op. cit.*, pp. 65–66.

3 *Ibid.*, p. 159, in Thurian, p. 46.

However, it is especially in the second book of Volume IV, in the chapter devoted to the second aspect of the atonement—redeemed humanity's elevation with and in Christ—that *Kirchliche Dogmatik* offers us significant aid in our problems here; Barth devotes to the subject a long parenthesis (eight pages), which we shall undertake to summarize here briefly.

Barth begins by recognizing the Reformers as right in their rejection of monasticism: monasticism was such at the end of the Middle Ages that it was necessary and in fact inevitable that it should be rejected, in accord with Reformation principles. This approval of the Reformer's attitude, however, is not to impede a favorable reception's being given present-day movements which attempt to reintroduce forms of religious-community life into the Church, while protecting themselves carefully, and specifically, against the abuses and distortions which historically justified the Reformation's severity.

Today, in fact, rather than reject en bloc the whole monastic movement, we should make an effort to distinguish between the fundamental impulses which underlay, and today still underlie, monastic or conventual undertakings and institutions, and the distortions which often very quickly were introduced into them, and still threaten to be introduced into them today.

What monasticism basically sought is not only acceptable, but clearly necessary in Christian life.

What monasticism, in its particular way, planned and undertook was a concrete method of following the Lord. Now following the Lord is something which in the Gospel we find required not only in general terms, but also described—in part at any rate, and as a model—in extremely precise detail. Here, then, is what was planned and undertaken: individual and collective sanctification, a way of Christian life designed for a purpose, a concrete and organic fraternal life, and all this under the impulse and in the service of a concrete and totall ove.[4]

This primary aim of monasticism was to be achieved by a combination of different factors. These factors Barth next undertakes to discuss, grouping them under three headings: solitude and flight from the world, practice of asceticism, and obedience.

Solitude, or flight from the world to enter a community, constitutes for Barth a kind of protest against the world and against a

4 *Kirchliche Dogmatik*, IV, ii, p. 13.

secularized Church. It is an expression, he feels, of the fact that a Christian is always at odds with this world. To this extent monasticism is a standing challenge to the Church:

> Can there be a Christian existence which does not have a need, greater or lesser, of a physical (not to say spiritual) distance from the world— and even from the Church—a distance which would still permit one to be bound to the world, to face up to it, to render it limitless service? This was in fact the dynamic distance which in the theory and practice of monasticism (even if mistaken) we have seen promoted to the level of a principle, a system, an objective law. Can the Church, and the individual, truly go out to meet the world, and men, without having to keep an all the truer distance from them? Is there not a need (arising from intrinsic as well as extrinsic necessities) to establish a pattern in which the place of the solitary life will always be assured?

This positive understanding of solitude or of distance from the world must not cause the dangers inherent therein to be overlooked. Sin is not connected with the things of this world except as man connects them; the solitary, if he takes nothing else with him into the desert, takes along temptation, and proneness to wrongdoing; nor can any place free him from what he bears within himself.

"Fleeing the world is nowise identical with fleeing to God." Furthermore, Christianity is not Manichaeism; for the Christian, the things of this world, matter, are not to be identified with evil.

The practice of asceticism, in Barth's view, is another element indispensable to Christian life, the aim of the practice being to resist one's passions so as to make one's self more free for the service of the Lord and one's fellow men. The new man created in faith by Jesus Christ must become a concrete figure in everyday life. Furthermore, ascesis signifies that "the fabric of this world dissolves" and that every Christian's attention should be focused on the end.

> One cannot leave out the question of Christian perfection, understood as an undeviating drive towards the goal, as the dynamism implied by the grace of God and contained necessarily in it, dynamism directed towards the service which this grace itself assigns to man.

And Barth adds this explanation:

> Monastic asceticism—in the midst of a Christianity which, from early and even earliest times, was always more or less a victim of de-emphasis on the Second Coming and of a secularization of its message and life—

was an implacable repetition of this question; and it was more—it was a tremendous drive towards an answer.[5]

Thus here too did monasticism offer its contribution to the whole of Christianity by emphasizing this question, which Barth explains in this way:

> We must ask ourselves . . . whether it is possible to lead the life of Christians with the liberty of Christians, and hence in the tension towards the goal which grace assigns to man; whether it is possible to undertake a service of God in spirit and in truth, and an authentic service of fellow men, and to manifest an aptitude for all this, without conducting a combat precisely in these fields—that is, without practicing a certain self-denial, a certain abstinence, and, in sum, without submitting one's self to a certain degree of mortification (even one without any plan or any submission to a rule, yet therefore all the more earnest). According to the Gospel, it is impossible. . . . Only one who can and will sacrifice can and will also serve, and free himself for this purpose.

This point once made, Barth directs severe criticism against the dangers included in asceticism, dangers to which, in his opinion, the monasticism of old in great part succumbed. The gravest danger consists in that of basing upon practices of mortification a state of life supposed to be higher than life conducted on the "ordinary" level, for this is to introduce, through ascetic practices, a division of the Church into two classes—the one of the perfect, the other of ordinary Christians. Furthermore—and this is more implicit than clearly expressed—there is the danger of making a salutary work out of ascetic practices, of finding in them a certain contributory aid in the acquisition of salvation, and hence of falling again under the Law.

Finally, obedience, too, has its dangers; there is the danger of confusing the authority of God with human authorities, and, in some degree, of identifying the two. Obedience understood in that way would seem to Barth an illusion, whereby some men would be given a superior, others an inferior, place. But it does not seem necessary to Barth that obedience be understood in that way; for him, it is possible to conceive monastic obedience as existing in the order of actualization and of love.

> To the extent that the monks and their rules made the institution of obedience and authority depend upon the actualization of the Holy Spirit, this obedience and this authority were sound.[6]

_____
5 *Ibid.*, p. 45.
6 *Ibid.*, p. 15.

Finally, monastic life, with its obedience, is a standing reminder that

> the communion of saints cannot be actualized save in the curious triangle made up of God and of two men bound together in a deliberate and fixed relationship.[7]

It would therefore be impossible to reject and condemn monasticism utterly; it is a sign of the Christian community—more specifically, of the actualization of the communion of saints, which is to say of the Church.

Besides, Barth believes that the basic intention which gave birth to so many monastic institutions in the past, and which still today, in Protestantism especially, is bringing about a rebirth of religious communities, is entirely acceptable from the point of view of the Gospel. The institution of conventual life means for him, in the final analysis, that faith, received through grace, implies the necessity of following Christ:

> It could then, and can now, be learned from monasticism that faith entails the necessity of following Christ, of walking in holiness, of giving a definite plan to Christian life, of putting fraternal life, and love, into formal practice.[8]

As for the individual orders, monasteries, and religious houses, both those of the past and those of the present, it must be seen in what way they are in fact translating into practice the basic intention which brought them into existence. Among the many elements in which this basic intention has sought realization, there may have easily slipped certain distortions, abuses, and errors. It may not be necessary to throw out the baby with the bath; but there may well be occasion for strict—though positive—criticism, aimed at purifying those various elements of whatever tends to distort and to compromise them.

Thus, while approving the Reformers' rejection of monasticism at the time of the Reformation because of the grave surrenders of principle which, in his opinion, had at that time submerged sound monasticism, Karl Barth—from what he considers the Gospel point of view (that is, in strict accordance with Protestantism)—justifies both the

---

7 *Ibid.*, p. 17.
8 *Loc. cit.*

fundamental principle of the monastic movement, and the actual monastic establishments which followed therefrom—to the extent, that is, that they remained faithful to that original orientation and to such elements as solitude, ascetic practices, and obedience, which are the logical sequels of that orientation. Indeed, it seems possible to go even farther: for Barth, even religious establishments gravely deficient in all those points might still have the value of a challenge to the Christian world. They are not to be rejected a priori, without a long critical examination.

To repeat, Karl Barth is not the whole of Protestantism, nor even the whole of Protestant theology. His is not the role of infallible teacher in the Reformed Church. His theological merit, and the part that he has played in the dogmatic awakening in Protestantism are incontestable. For that reason, his judgment on the question of monasticism (especially on the question of the present-day forms that the Protestant cenobitical movement has taken) enables us to answer the question proposed with a measure of assurance. It is indeed within Protestantism, and in accord, not with the letter, but with the spirit of the Reformers, that Protestant religious communities have a right to exist today.

PROSPECT

We have arrived at the end of our study of Continental communities. We are keenly aware that our work here is incomplete, for it is limited, first of all, to a consideration of only some Reformers— Luther, Calvin, Melanchthon, Zwingli, Bucer—and then to only some of their works. It has dealt with only some of the religious foundations undertaken in former centuries, and only some of those existing today; nor does it include all the arguments of Protestant theologians in favor of religious common life.

Yet despite this incompleteness it leads us rather clearly to the conclusion that in present-day Protestant monasticism (to use, as we have been doing, the traditional word, though strictly speaking it would be subject to a number of qualifications) there is something *new*, both in contrast with the virtually negative position of the Reformers on this matter, and in contrast with what might be called the typical Protestant tradition.

For in general Protestantism held fast to the attitudes of the Reformers on religious life, and average Protestantism does so still today. Commonly forgetting the few favorable opinions that persisted in Reformation theologians' criticism—they were indeed few, as we have seen—the average Protestant simply does not know that in the history of the Churches brought into being by the Reformation a certain number of major thinkers—like Kierkegaard, and even Harnack—were not nearly so categorical in the judgments they expressed on monasticism and the religious life.[1]

---

1 Harnack wrote, for example, in his *Wesen des Christentums*, 1900 edition, p. 180: "The Reformation suppressed monasticism; it could do no other. It was

We call the modern movement something new also in contrast with the various attempts made in this line during the preceding centuries, within the Protestant world. This is quite clear in the case of groups like the Moravian Brethren: they were basically much more like parishes with a lively community spirit than like religious communities properly so called. Of course a community like that of the Pilgerhüte, founded under the influence of Teerstegen, comes closer to the present-day forms. But, besides its being an experiment rather than a truly stable institution, the rule followed there seems a collection of directives in the line of piety and meditation, rather than of principles of religious common life properly speaking.

The deaconess movement of the nineteenth century also presents certain aspects of the religious life. In fact, the deaconesses were expressly founded in order to constitute a body of Protestant Sisters of Charity. Nevertheless—though this judgment is in need of several qualifications—the final goal of this foundation seems to have been a number of *services* of misfortunate fellow men, and the community life a means for the more ready achievement of this goal.

In present-day Protestant communities the primary and basic aim is life in common according to the principles of the Gospel. Work for the Church, services, ministry—these are not excluded, naturally;

---

right in considering life-long ascetic vows temerarious. It was right in considering every vocation in the world, worked out under the eye of God, as of equal value with the monastic state. But then there happened what Luther had neither forseen nor wished: indispensable monasticism, conceived in conformity with the Gospel, disappeared completely. But any kind of community calls for some persons who devote themselves exclusively to it. Thus the Church calls for volunteers who abandon every other calling—"renounce the world"—and devote themselves wholly to the service of their neighbor, not because such a vocation is higher, but simply because it is necessary, and because such an impetus will necessarily come from a Church that is truly living. But the hardening-over of anti-Catholicism prevented the hatching of such a vocation in the Protestant Churches. Here was too high a price for us to pay, and one not made up for by the mere flowering of simple, everyday piety within the family home."

Kierkegaard wrote the following lines in his journal (*Tagebücher*, Häcker edition, 1948): "No doubt on this point: our times especially in Protestantism call for the reinstitution of religious community life. . . . The convent is an essential dynamic factor in Christianity; it is like a pointer to indicate to us what we are."

but they are taken up by communities already constituted on other grounds. In other words, these exist first of all as communities, for the purpose of life in common in accordance with the requirements of the Gospel, before conducting this or that ministry, or devoting themselves to this or that activity.

Besides, they habitually follow a rule which contains the principles of religious community life. In most cases the members of these communities bind themselves to them by "commitments," the form and description of which vary, indeed, from community to community, but which constitute one of the uniform features of the most vigorous foundations existing today.

In the case of some of these foundations, dare one not go further still, and note a certain "surpassing" of the Reformers? We have noted—following Karl Barth, and abiding by his opinion—that these communities are acceptable to Protestantism. But is this not on the condition of not limiting Protestantism to a doctrine established at the time of the Reformation? Is it not on the condition of also admitting that in the Protestant Churches themselves, and in Protestant theology as well, critical judgment is brought to play upon the Reformation and its attitudes, even the most emphatically maintained of these? That it is in this way that the most open-minded and most alert Protestantism conceives itself is something we may gladly concede. Therefore we may say that it seems that present-day communities, quite authentically Protestant though they be, provide a criticism —by their life itself, but also through their undertakings in the field of theological thought—of Reformation attitudes, and that in several cases this criticism leads to a revision, nay even to a rejection of certain of those attitudes.

Something new, but—we must strongly emphasize—something extremely rare, now and doubtless for a long time to come. In the whole of Protestantism the religious communities can be easily counted on one's fingers. They are found neither outside European Protestantism nor in all the countries of Europe. The authorities in various Churches are gingerly in accepting such institutions. Even if they esteem their value and their interest, it is only with serious reservations that they count them a part of the real furniture of the Church. The great body of Protestants have very little time for such undertakings, and indeed a large number of them are simply unaware of the fact that religious communities exist in their Churches.

Catholics, on the other hand, must be under no illusion here. From facts like those reported in this volume, from unequivocal evidence of the rebirth of the Church spirit in Protestantism, and from the currents of thought which are emphasizing the importance of the Eucharist and the sacraments, Catholics, with admirable generosity and receptiveness, may be tempted to conclude that here indeed are harbingers of an early return of Protestantism to Catholicism.

There is in present-day Protestantism a new attention to and a re-surgence of elements[2] which have always existed in Catholicism. And there are met today, in the Churches that sprang from the Reforma-tion, certain elements that have always enriched the Eastern Church —liturgy, monasticism. That much is certain, and by no Catholic may it be ignored. Thanks be for it to the Spirit of God, who has thus inspired our separated brothers.

At the same time there is no use succumbing to a blind optimism. These various aspects of Church rebirth are not the whole of Protes-tantism; much less dare we identify the Protestant Churches with the High Church currents which appear within them. Protestantism is a phenomenon far too complex to allow us to conclude from certain Catholicizing, or even simply liturgical or sacramentarian, currents to a disappearance or even a diminution of those rejections and denials which make it opposed to what Catholicism basically affirms.

Is this the same as saying that the ecumenical interests of the Protestant religious communities are of little account? Not for a moment do we think so. Quite to the contrary, we are persuaded that, in ecumenical relations, such communities play a highly im-portant part.

This ecumenical function is evident first of all in the fact—already emphasized in the third part of this book—that the Protestant com-munities are all, or nearly all, centers of contact for Christians of different faiths. The importance of actual exchange of thoughts and of direct conversation will hardly escape anyone: to understand other Christian faiths, to discover their spiritual bents, to recognize in them the Christian values and wealth that the Spirit of Christ maintains

---

2 But in ways quite diverse, and not without the admixture of other elements.

or develops in them, despite what appear to others as errors and objective deficiencies—nothing can substitute here for personal contact. Father Couturier, it will be recalled, was awakened to a sense of Christian unity through cordial relationships with the fervent Orthodox Russian refugees at Lyons. Doubtless many Christians first discovered the prayer and the work that are going on for the achievement of unity when they came for a retreat, a stay, or simply a visit in one of these communities.

More fundamentally, the Protestant religious community movement throws a strong light on one certain method of ecumenicism; it shows its efficaciousness.

As we have explained, the founders of the Protestant communities have not undertaken to imitate Catholic religious orders or to transplant Eastern monasticism into Protestantism. It was by meditation on the Gospel and the requirements it contains that certain men and women of good will heard the call of the Lord to a certain original form of life, breaking with the world in giving up certain things amidst which other Christians are called to live their faith. It is likewise by meditation on the Gospel-based requirements of community life itself that these new foundations bit by bit advanced towards a discovery of the fundamental elements of religious common life: celibacy, obedience, and common ownership of property.

In our opinion there are signs here of an ecumenical method very rich in promise. The ecumenical effort must surely entail the desire to see realized in one's own faith whatever seems good in other faiths. There is in this an aspect of the spiritual emulation which Father Couturier had occasion to praise. This kind of imitation is not, however, without grave dangers. There is the danger, so to speak, of plastering certain practices on a confessional structure ill prepared for such an application. Each Christian faith, in fact, is a whole, whose various elements are bound together by a certain organic logic, and by a certain "tradition." Transplanting a flowering growth from one faith to another may be simply trying to root it in a location where in various ways it is bound to remain out of place.

Furthermore, this imitation of one another by religious faiths, which may be sometimes serviceable, still does not seem wholly worthwhile unless it is accompanied by a deepened appreciation of the authentic values contained in each of these faiths—values which can be developed through the adoption of such and such an element of liturgy, worship, Church organization, or religious mentality that other faiths have kept and developed.

It seems to us that, without being a prophet, one may still say that by an increasingly deeper study of the requirements contained in the Gospel each faith will come to perceive, within itself, the conditions for the unity desired by the Lord for his Church, conditions which we Roman Catholics recognize as substantially realized in the Church of Rome. Of course, various causes may play their part in the way towards unity; they are not all of a religious or theological kind. But the essential one remains specifically religious, or better yet directly evangelical. It is up to the Christian faiths to discern—on the basis of what they hold in common, namely, recognition of Jesus Christ as Lord and Savior—the fundamental principles which will enable them to dissolve the barriers that separate them. This entails perceiving the form of unity expressed in Revelation, to be determined by a more profound study of the Word of God and doubtless by a new close reading of the biblical texts, over and beyond the interpretations of the Reformation. Ecumenical interchange indeed seems fated to be a sterile academic discussion unless it succeeds in directing the attention of all to the Lord's own requirements in the matter of unity.

The renaissance of religious communities in Protestantism, and their development, emphasizes the spiritual efficaciousness of this method.

By the Spirit of the Lord, as it seems to us, fervent Christians have been awakened in the Churches born of the Reformation to a form of service, recommendation of which they have found in the very texts which have always been most dear to their particular tradition, and especially in the Gospel itself. It is in listening to the Lord speak to them through what their own Churches have handed down to them that they have heard his call, and have tried to respond to their vocation.

Here now, surely, is a sign and an example of which Christians should be aware when attempting to determine the direction of their own effort towards unity—a sign and an example to help them preserve, in the face of the difficulties of the ecumenical undertaking, both hope and joy.

INDEX

159